Dukan Diet

Delicious Recipes To Help You Lose Weight

By Linda Matthews and Michael Westwood

CONTENTS

Introduction

Dieting is the most common and popular approach followed by the majority of people who are looking to shed those extra pounds of flesh. Obesity and other related issues are becoming a primary issue with today's generation all over the world. There are a variety of dietary approaches available, each of which has their own pros and cons. It is true that most of these diets result in weight loss, but there is one issue that most people face. Close to 95 percent of people who lost weight when they followed a diet, started to gain weight when they switched back to their old eating routine.

Is there a way to tackle this issue? Yes, with the Dukan Diet method! What is the Dukan method of dieting? Is there anything special about this diet when compared to other dietary approaches?

The Dukan Diet, designed by the French Dietician and nutritionist, Pierre Dukan, is a protein-based eating pattern. In this diet, you are required to follow an eating pattern that was followed by the cavemen. You must regularly consume food that is rich in protein. This diet pattern allows you to eat 100 food items out of which 28 are derived from plants while 72 are animal food sources.

There are no restrictions on the amount of food one can consume when they follow this diet. You can eat as much as you want as long as you stick to the food list. The benefits of the diet haven't been confirmed by any research, and there is an ongoing debate on whether this dietary plan is indeed beneficial to human health.

The Dukan Diet can help in to stabilize your weight permanently by helping you redesign your eating patterns or habits.

So, what is a Dukan Diet? It is a high protein, low-carb and low-fat diet that comprises of a variety of vegetables and protein-rich food items that can be consumed. The diet follows the *"eat as much as you like"* concept, but within the choice of the 100 defined food list. This diet does not guarantee you instant or excessive results in a particular time. Instead, the diet will help you achieve your ideal weight (realistic number as per your BMI). Not only can you attain your ideal weight, but you can also maintain it for the rest of your life.

According to Dukan Dietary method, you lose weight if you consume loads of protein because,

- You feel satiated for an extended period and therefore don't overeat or binge
- Your body needs more energy to digest the protein thereby ensuring that the stored fat is burnt to produce the extra energy
- Since your diet is rich in protein, your caloric intake reduces since protein-rich food are low in calories

When you restrict the consumption of fats and carbohydrates, you are forcing your body to shift into the starvation state where it is deprived of glucose (primary fuel for energy). This forces the body to use stored fat to produce energy. You must exercise regularly and also consume whole foods.

In this book, we will discuss the Dukan Diet and its four phases. The chapters in this book will help you understand more about the Dukan Diet, its history, steps to follow, foods you can eat and some important guidelines pertaining to the diet. The book also helps you with a diet plan that can be followed during the first few weeks and some delicious Dukan Diet recipes included in the book.

Chapter One: The Dukan Diet

Pierre Dukan, a French nutritionist, designed the Dukan Diet in 2000 when one of his friends, who was severely obese, approached him regarding treatment. He then designed this diet to help his friend lose weight quickly. When his friend followed the diet for a week, he lost ten pounds and did not gain any weight when he returned to his old pattern of eating.

What sets this diet apart from every other diet? The Dukan Diet allows you to consume unlimited quantities of food with the only restriction being you consume the food mentioned in the approved list. The following are the rules of the Dukan Diet:

- Drink plenty of water
- Eat oat bran regularly
- Consume as much lean protein as possible
- Exercise or take a 20-minute walk regularly

When you follow the Dukan Diet, you deprive your body of carbohydrates thereby depriving your body of glucose leading to the starvation state. In the starvation state, the body burns the stored fat to produce energy.

History of The Dukan Diet

The Dukan method of eating pattern is dubbed as the medical solution of the French to permanent weight loss. This dietary approach adheres to an eating prescription. It comes with four phases, and you are allowed to choose from the 72 approved food items in the first phase. Carbs are a strict NO, even if they come from vegetables and fruit.

The high-protein, low-carb and low-fat dietary plan was initially published in France in 2000 by Pierre Dukan and was called *"**Je ne sais pas maigrir**"* (I don't know how to lose weight). Not many knew about this diet until it was rebranded as the Dukan Diet in the UK around 2010. The Dukan movement was followed by a few people in France, but the moment it reached the UK it became a miracle weight-loss diet routine.

The Dukan Diet was not highly marketed, but it was taking over the world slowly. Kate Middleton was said to have dropped two dress sizes after she followed the Dukan Diet before her royal wedding.

Pierre Dukan specialized in neurology and was practicing in that field. He switched to the field of nutrition when a high-protein diet he designed for a friend worked wonders. As mentioned earlier, a friend of his approached him with a severe obesity disorder, and Dukan recommended a high-protein, low-carb diet to him. When he next saw his friend, he was surprised by the quick reduction in his size. This development motivated him to work on the diet plan and design it with care. He spent time on research and developed a plan where the food consumed in the diet was nutritious. Eventually, the success of the dietary approach made him popular in his country, and he published a book about the diet. The Dukan Diet book soon became a bestseller, and has, until today, sold more than seven million copies. The book has also been translated into 14 different languages.

The dietary approach designed by the Frenchman did attract quite a bit of controversy when many health experts criticized the diet pattern as an unhealthy and unbalanced way of eating. These controversial claims affected not only Pierre Dukan's diet plan, but also the brand – Dukan.

When you look at the science behind the Dukan method, it will sound similar to the Ketogenic diet, since both dietary approaches concentrate on reducing or completely eliminating carbohydrates from the diet. The Keto diet follows a high fat, moderate protein and low carb dietary approach while the Dukan Diet follows a high protein, low fat, and low carb dietary approach.

The body primarily uses glucose, which is obtained from carbohydrates, to produce energy. But, when you follow the keto diet, you deprive your body of carbohydrates thereby reducing the percentage of glucose available in the body. The body then burns the stored fat to produce energy pushing your body into a metabolic state called ketosis. Though this does give you the required effect for weight loss, continuously pushing your body to ketosis for long periods may cause problems to your health. The Dukan Diet does not cause your body to shift into the state of ketosis since there is no restriction on the quantity of food you are allowed to consume.

Dukan Diet and its four phases

The high-protein, low–carb and low-fat weight loss diet is believed to encourage quick weight loss while reducing the pangs of hunger. The diet has four phases that must be followed to gain effective results. The first two phases aid in weight loss phases while the remaining two phases help to maintain the weight.

You must begin the diet once you have calculated your ideal weight based on your weight loss journey, age, height, and other factors. The number of days you need to stay in each phase depends on your current weight and the number of pounds you must lose to reach your ideal weight.

The four phases of the Dukan Dietary approach are:

- The Attack Phase
- The Cruise Phase
- The Consolidation Phase
- The Stabilization Phase

The Attack phase

The Attack phase lasts for a week or ten days (depending on your ideal weight). You are allowed to consume only pure protein food to kick-start your weight-loss program.

There are close to 72 protein-rich food you can eat to generate quick and obvious weight loss results. You can see results within a week if you keep to the rules of this phase. You shouldn't eat any carbs but only protein-rich food.

You are allowed to eat an unlimited quantity of lean protein along with 1 1/2 tablespoons of oat bran every day. Your water intake should be a minimum of 6 cups every day.

The Cruise Phase

The Cruise phase is where you focus on your weight loss and observe the weight you lose regularly until you reach your ideal weight. The phase can last from 1 month to a year depending on your goal. Along with the existing list of 72 protein-rich foods, you need to add 28 vegetables to your food platter.

You must alternate between protein-rich food and vegetables + protein-rich food. As days go by, you will slowly but steadily lose weight and reach your ideal weight. You should not consume carbs on your protein-only days but can consume a small portion of carbohydrates on other days.

You must continue to consume lean protein on protein-only days and include an unlimited amount of non-starchy vegetables along with lean protein on vegetable plus protein days. You must also consume two tablespoons of oat bran every day (this is an extra half tablespoon more than your previous phase).

The Consolidation phase

The consolidation phase is the most important phase since your body is vulnerable and has the tendency to regain the lost weight quickly. You need to thwart the rebound effect, and this phase is designed to do exactly that. You need to slowly introduce the prohibited food to your diet in limited quantities and have only two celebration meals (eat anything you want with a bit of restriction) during a week. You must continue this phase until you do not see any gain in weight.

An important point to note is that you must only consume protein-rich food on one day during the week, preferably Thursday. On the other days, you are free to eat fruit, one serving of hard cheese, starchy vegetables (one or two servings), a bit of carb, some fats, two slices of whole-grain bread and unlimited lean protein. Your consumption of oat bran should be increased to 2.5 tablespoons per day.

The Stabilization phase

The stabilization phase is crucial, and you must follow this for the remainder of your life. If you have successfully reintroduced carbs into your diet without putting on weight, you are free to step into the last phase of the Dukan Diet. You now know your body's capability and its reaction to the food you eat, so you will need to consciously continue to follow a healthy eating pattern.

There are three crucial but basic rules you must follow:

- 20-minutes regular walking (avoid using lifts and take stairs whenever possible)
- Thursday should be a pure-protein day (follow your attack phase menu)
- Three tablespoons oat bran daily

If you strictly adhere to the rules and guidelines given in each of these phases, you will most likely reach your ideal weight and maintain it without regaining the lost weight.

	Attack	Cruise	Consolidation	Stabilization
Food choices	72 proteins	Plus 28 vegetables	Plus whole grain bread, fruit, cheese, and starchy foods	Include the foods from all the groups
Expected weight loss	2 to 8 pounds during phase	2 pounds per week on average		
Duration	7 to 10 days	About 3 days per pound	About 5 days per pound lost in Cruise	Rest of your life
Oat bran to be consumed (Tablespoon /day)	1.5	2	2	3
Physical activity (duration/day)	20 min	30 min	25 min	20 min

What is the difference between The Dukan Diet and Atkins Diet?

You don't need to count your carbs, nutritional values or calories while you follow the Dukan Diet. All you must do is choose from the offered list of approved food items in the first three phases and add a few more (depending on your old eating routine) in the last phase. Dukan Diet specifically concentrates on low-fat protein, which includes non-fat dairy products while the Atkins diet gives you unlimited access to meat fats, any saturated fats or dairy fats. In Atkins diet, you can eat packaged foods; shakes and bars while Dukan focuses only on the 100 approved natural foods (strictly no packaged foods). You can also consume unlimited quantities of food from the approved list of vegetables and protein foods.

Does The Dukan Diet really work?

Health experts and critics point out that the Dukan Diet completely bans a specific group of foods such as grains, fruit and starchy vegetables that make the diet incomplete in nutrition. You are most likely to observe a good amount of weight loss during your first and second phase. But, the moment you reach your ideal weight and return to your usual eating routine, there are chances that you may regain the weight lost in the first phase.

Though research shows that high-protein diets are effective for weight loss, experts do not accept The Dukan Diet since they are concerned about the long-term effects of the diet. Moreover, there is no evidence that a regular 20-minute walk and one all-protein day is enough to maintain your ideal weight and prevent you from gaining weight.

The diet has also been criticized, as it is quite difficult and inconvenient to adhere to the rules of the phases. If not followed properly, you tend to gain the weight back, which will force you to start from scratch. The other issues with the maintenance phase are:

- Only water weight is lost in the first phase of the diet
- Rules are stringent and can make the diet difficult or boring to follow
- Eating lean protein (fish and meat) regularly can turn into a costly affair

According to the National Health Service (NHS) in the United Kingdom, "*Ultimately, a diet that is as restrictive as the Dukan Diet will result in weight loss simply due to a calorie deficit as a result of limited food choices, boredom and lack of enjoyment from eating.*"

Since there is no research that can be used to support the claim that the high-protein diet is effective and safe, it is always better to speak to a doctor first before you proceed further. The official Dukan Diet website also advises the same.

Chapter Two: Tips and Guidelines

You will be motivated and happy when you see that you are losing weight during the initial attack phase. If you are someone who doesn't like to keep counting the intake of calories, then the Dukan Diet is for you! The diet is preferred by many because it has a prescriptive approach to eating and gives you the list of food you can have during each phase of the dietary plan.

The Dukan Diet restricts the consumption of fats and prohibits the intake of vegetables in any form during the first phase. The subsequent phases of the diet gradually allow you to reintroduce a few carbs, vegetables (non-starchy in the second phase and starchy in the third phase) and certain fruit. According to certain reports, it is the last phase of the diet that sometimes causes the most problems due to the following reasons:

- The dieters find it challenging to re-introduce their old eating habits without gaining weight

- Sticking to the all-protein day once a week is difficult

The sustainability and the effectiveness of the French diet have not been proved, as there is limited scientific support for the same. Though people do lose quite a bit of weight (actually more) during the initial strict phases of the diet, many of them regain the weight they lost by returning to their old eating habits. A survey showed that around 80 percent of the dieters regained their lost weight within four years.

As pointed out by many health experts, the dietary approach doesn't encourage healthy eating as it almost excludes the vegetables, fiber, whole grains and fruit during the diet phase. These dieters do not gain the benefits of all these healthy food items, which ultimately result in a nutrition imbalance.

This restrictive low-carb diet can cause certain side effects during the start of the diet, and some might even face other issues on a long-term basis.

- The low levels of carbs in the body for a long period can cause fatigue, dizziness, and lack of energy
- Some dieters might have dry mouth and bad breath during the initial phases of the diet
- The low levels of fiber in the body might lead to potential bowel issues and constipation in some.
- The restricted choice of food can cause nutrition deficiency
- Some might gain weight around the waist area toward the end of the diet

Irrespective of whatever diet you follow, it is necessary to check with your dietician or physician before you go in for a diet change.

What are the foods you can eat on the Dukan Diet?

Attack phase

This phase of the diet is strictly only-protein food zone and is mainly based on protein-dense food items along with few other minimal calorie-foods. You can eat the following foods during this phase:

- Eggs
- Lean pork
- Tongue, liver, kidney
- Skinless poultry
- Fish and all types of shellfish
- Bison, lean beef, veal
- Seitan (made from gluten – meat substitute)
- Non-fat dairy products (only 32 ounces per day) – ricotta cheese, yogurt, cottage cheese, milk
- 1.5 tablespoons of oat bran every day (mandatory)
- Tempeh and Tofu
- Minimum 1.5 liters of water every day
- Not more than 1 teaspoon of oil for greasing
- Shirataki noodles, diet gelatin, and unlimited artificial sweeteners
- Little amounts of pickles and lemon juice

Cruise phase

You have to alternate your days between full-protein food one day and vegetables plus protein the next. This needs to be continued alternating every day.

You will need to consume only the food items that are listed in the attack phase during your full-protein day and on your day two; you can eat the attack phase foods along with the following vegetables:

- Artichokes
- Bell peppers
- Lettuce, Spinach, leafy greens and kale
- Asparagus
- Cauliflower, Brussels sprouts, and Broccoli
- Cucumbers
- Tomatoes
- Eggplant
- Celery
- Spaghetti squash
- Mushrooms
- Turnips
- Green beans
- Shallots, onions, and leeks
- Pumpkin
- Two tablespoons of oat bran every day (mandatory)
- One serving of beets or carrots regularly
- 1 teaspoon of oil for greasing or salad dressing (strictly no fats)

You shouldn't be using any other fruit or vegetables apart from the ones mentioned above.

Consolidation Phase

The dieters are allowed to mix and match the list of food options from the first two phases along with the following food list in the consolidation phase.

- Two celebration meals in a week that can include a main dish, a glass of wine, an appetizer and a dessert
- One to two servings of starches in a week – corn, legumes, potatoes, 8 ounces of pasta, beans, rice or other grains
- Two whole grain bread slices in a day (if you want you can spread a small amount of no-fat or reduced-fat butter or other spreads)
- One serving (1.5 ounces) of cheese in a day
- One serving of fruit in a day
    o Two apricots, kiwis or plums
    o One medium pear, apple, nectarine, orange or pear
    o Chopped melon
    o 1 cup berries
- 2.5 tablespoons of oat bran regularly (mandatory)
- Roasted meat once or twice in a week
- One pure protein day in a week (food from the attack phase is only allowed)

Stabilization phase

The final phase of the diet doesn't involve many new introductions of food items but rather concentrates on maintaining the achieved improvement from the first three phases of the diet. You don't have a strict off-limits on any food but quite a few rules to be followed to ensure you don't get back your lost weight.

- You can plan your regular meals by using the third phase as your basic framework
- Walk more. No elevators or lifts, only stairs!
- Continue taking oat bran regularly – 3 tablespoons!
- Don't stop the pure protein-day concept. You need to dedicate one day just to proteins every week.

Can everyone follow this diet?

It is true that one can witness immediate and rapid weight loss when the Dukan Diet is followed, but for certain people with specific health conditions, the benefits may be overshadowed by the risks involved.

- If you are a diabetic on medication, then you might have to check with your doctor and increase the dosage when you are on this diet as the carb intake will be very low during the first two phases
- If you have a kidney issue or other renal disease, then the amount of protein you will be consuming in this diet will affect your kidneys as it would be more for them to handle
- If you have gut issues or digestive disorder or heart complaints, then this diet will not suit you as there are no heart-healthy fiber in the diet
- If you are above 50, talk to a doctor before proceeding with the diet.

This is the reason I keep reiterating to check with your doctor or dietician before you proceed with this diet as the dietary pattern is restrictive regarding the food intake (nutrients). If you have to lose a lot of weight to reach your ideal weight, then the diet may go for months or maybe years. And if it takes too long a time, you may develop health issues (especially if you are not great health-wise), as the diet is inadequate in terms of nutrition.

If you have to lose only a small amount of weight, then this diet can help you with rapid weight loss.

Chapter Three: Getting Started

Before you begin with the Dukan Diet, you will want to consider:

- **Calculate your ideal weight**

It is essential to know your ideal weight to define how long you must follow certain phases. The first three phases of the diet are crucial for your weight loss

- **Understand why you want to lose weight**

It is important that you answer this question, so you understand the reasons behind why you want to lose weight. Take it slow, one step at a time. Write down your reasons to encourage you to achieve your ideal weight and help you stick to the routine.

- **Have a chat with your physician or dietician**

Before you go ahead with your diet plans, talk to your doctor. It would be a good idea to have a complete checkup – blood pressure, thyroid checkup, cholesterol level details, stress test, etc.

- **Talk to your family and friends**

Take time to explain the importance of your weight loss plan
to them. Tell them how essential it is for them to
provide their support to help you reach your goal.

- **Finalize your start date**

Once you are done with all the necessary discussions and
planning, give yourself a head start by deciding the
start day. Let's say – Sunday! This will make you
realize that this is a task-driven approach, and
therefore, you need to be serious about it

- **Clear your kitchen and stock it with Dukan-approved foods**

Check your kitchen cabinets, your refrigerator, and your
pantry. Clear away the foods that might tempt you to
cheat on your diet. Stock your pantry with the 100
approved food list.

How difficult is the process?

The process isn't really complicated or tough – the level of
effort is pretty medium. Since you already have the food list,
preparing your own food shouldn't be a big problem. There
are no hard-to-find or exotic ingredients for your dishes. The
only thing that may seem difficult initially is to adhere to the
food list during the first phase of the diet.

You can get tired of eating oat bran every single day.
Consuming only protein-rich food may become monotonous
and boring too. Shopping and cooking shouldn't be too much
of an issue since it is quite easy to plan your shopping items

based on your weekly meal plan. No packaged food or no eating outside! Walking regularly for twenty minutes is mandatory, and this step shouldn't be skipped.

Are there any dietary preferences or restrictions?

A vegan or vegetarian can follow this diet, but it can get boring since you won't have too many options to choose from as nuts, beans and lentils come under prohibited food list in the first phase. Tofu, Seitan and Tempeh are the only veggie options that are available to you. The first phase of the diet is entirely into the consumption of poultry, seafood, eggs, lean meat, and fat-free dairy.

If you have a heart condition that forces you to eat extremely low-fat foods or if you are already on a low-fat diet routine, then this diet is a perfect fit for you since vegetables, protein and fruit are the only food allowed and all of them are low-fat, lean or no-fat.

If you are used to following a gluten-free eating pattern, the diet may fit you during the initial phases, but as you get to the third phase, it is not a strict gluten-free diet. It is, therefore, better to read the labels of the food items before you consume.

Sample meal plan for the first three phases

Attack phase

Breakfast

- 1.5 tablespoons oat bran, cinnamon, non-fat cottage cheese, and artificial sweetener
- Black tea or coffee with artificial sweetener (or you can add a bit of non-fat milk)
- Water

Lunch

- Diet gelatin
- Roast chicken
- Shirataki noodles
- Iced coffee

Dinner

- Lean meat and seafood (maybe lean beef and salmon)
- Decaf tea or coffee (with or without non-fat milk) and sweetener
- Water
- Diet gelatin

Cruise phase

Breakfast

- Sliced tomatoes or cucumber
- Scrambled eggs (2 or 3)
- Coffee with non-fat milk and sweetener
- Water

Lunch

- Iced tea
- Grilled chicken with leafy greens

- 2 tablespoons of oat bran with Greek yogurt and sweetener

Dinner

- Diet gelatin
- Baked salmon
- Decaf coffee with non-fat milk and sweetener
- Steamed cauliflower

Consolidation phase

Breakfast

- Egg omelet with 1.5 ounces of ricotta cheese and spinach (you can use three eggs)
- Water
- Black coffee with or without sweetener

Lunch

- Chicken sandwich on two whole wheat bread slices
- 2.5 tablespoons oat bran, cinnamon, half cup cheese and sweetener
- Iced tea

Dinner

- Grilled zucchini and steamed broccoli
- 1 apple (medium)
- Roasted meat
- Water
- Decaf coffee with sweetener and non-fat milk

Available research and studies on the diet

Though there aren't many quality researches available on this high-protein diet, there was one particular study done on Polish women. The ladies who followed the diet claimed that they lost close to 33 pounds within ten weeks by consuming 100 grams of protein and 1000 calories every day. That is, like 15 kg weight loss in 10 weeks!

There are many more studies that show low-carb and high-protein diets do have a major impact on rapid weight loss. Although there are several factors that contribute to the beneficial effects these protein-specific diets have on weight-loss routine, the important factor is gluconeogenesis.

When your body doesn't find enough glucose, it turns to protein and fat to convert it into energy. The result of high-protein intake forces the body to burn body fat in the process known as gluconeogenesis. This ultimately results in a higher number of calories being burned during the diet process.

The metabolic rate of your body increases when you eat more protein, and it makes you feel satiated for a longer period. Increase in protein naturally decreases the secretion of hunger hormones (ghrelin) thereby boosting satiety hormones such as PYY, CCK, and GLP-1. You basically don't eat more!

Since the Dukan Diet strictly restricts both fats and carbs, it is different from many other high-protein diets (like Paleo). There is no science behind restricting fat on a high-protein and low-carb diet especially when it comes to health and weight-loss. There was a study conducted on people who consumed fat along with high-protein but a low-carb meal.

They were able to burn more calories (on an average 69) than the ones who avoided fat too.

Though consuming oat bran is mandatory in the Dukan Diet, the initial phase of the diet is still low in fiber as there is only 5 grams or lesser amount of fiber in 1.5 to 2 tablespoons of oat bran. And such a small amount doesn't really provide any health benefits. Nuts and avocados that are rich sources of fiber aren't included in the diet as they are high in fat as well.

Safety of the diet and the health risks it poses

As mentioned earlier, the safety of the diet hasn't been studied extensively yet. Few other health risks that you may encounter if you follow the diet for an extended period are:

- Impact on bone and kidney health due to the consumption of protein-rich food
- People with weak kidneys or kidney stones may find that their condition has worsened
- Threat to bone density and health. However, the threat can be reduced if you include high-potassium fruit and vegetables along with your high-protein diet
- People with liver diseases should consult a doctor before proceeding further.

Though the diet gives you results on your weight-loss journey, it unnecessarily forces you to avoid many healthy nutritious foods, which might cause issues at a later stage.

Chapter Four: Frequently Asked Questions

Am I allowed to consume any quantity of food?

Yes, you are allowed to consume any quantity of protein-rich food. However, there is a restriction on the number of eggs you can consume. You are only allowed to consume two eggs with yolk during the week and unlimited egg whites.

Can I consume lentils and split peas on protein days?

Split peas aren't allowed until the third phase (consolidation phase). Two tablespoons of lentils per day is allowed on pure protein days (only if you are a vegan or vegetarian).

Can I consume alcohol when on the diet?

No alcohol until the third phase (consolidation phase).

What are the beverages I am allowed?

You can drink both iced and hot coffee and tea without sugar. You can drink milk and other dairy beverages as long as they are fat-free, low-carb and have low sugar. Calorie-free and sugar-free diet sodas and beverages are allowed. Club soda, sparkling water or seltzer can also be consumed.

Can I snack between my meals?

You are allowed to eat an unlimited amount of snacks as long as the ingredients are within the approved 100-food list.

Are carrots and beets allowed in this diet?

Though both these root vegetables are well known for their sugar content, in reality, they don't contain a high amount of sugar. However, the sugar in the vegetables can be absorbed by your body and transferred to the bloodstream especially when they are cooked. You can eat these vegetables as long as you don't cook with added fat, dressing or sauce.

I seem to have trouble sleeping since the time I started with the diet. Is there a reason why?

Though there is no direct connection between insomnia and Dukan Diet, we have heard this complaint from most of the dieters. Consuming a lot of coffee, tea. and other caffeine-rich beverages can be the reason. Your body is more sensitive to caffeine since you are consuming fewer carbs. It is therefore advised to go for decaffeinated versions of beverages. If you are really addicted to coffee and tea, try reducing the amount to take in daily.

Chapter Five: Attack Phase Recipes

Chicken and Herb Omelet Sandwich

Servings: 1

Type: Breakfast

Ingredients:

- 1 cooked and shredded chicken breast
- 3 eggs
- 1 tablespoon parsley (chopped)
- 1 1/2 tablespoon mixed herbs (chopped) – you can use basil, oregano, rosemary, thyme and chives
- 1 tablespoon cream cheese (fat-free)
- 3 tablespoons oat bran
- 2 tablespoons plain Greek yogurt (fat-free)
- 1 teaspoon baking powder
- Olive oil, for greasing

Method:

1. Take a rectangular bowl and combine the yogurt, baking powder, oat bran, and one egg together. Beat the mixture well until blended completely
2. Add the chopped parsley to the egg-yogurt mixture and microwave it on high for 4 minutes.
3. Remove the bowl from the microwave and let it cool. The mixture should get solidified to the texture of bread.
4. Slice the bread into two pieces and toast it lightly so that they don't get over dry.
5. Take a small bowl and beat the remaining two eggs. Add the chopped mixed herbs and mix it well.
6. Use few drops of olive oil to grease a non-stick frying pan and heat it over medium-high heat.
7. Pour the beaten egg-herb mixture into the hot pan and let the omelet cook for 5 minutes
8. Fold the cooked omelet on four sides to make a rectangle
9. Take one toasted bread slice and spread the cream cheese on it.
10. Place the shredded cooked chicken on the spread cheese, add the cooked omelet and then place the next slice of bread.
11. Your sandwich is ready. Serve immediately and enjoy!

Sausage Egg Breakfast

Servings: 1

Type: Breakfast

Ingredients:

- 1 sliced breakfast sausage (Frozen)
- 1 egg
- 2 scrambled egg whites
- 1 ounce cheddar cheese (crumbled)
- Olive oil, for greasing

Method:
1. Take a small bowl and crack the egg in it. Beat it well.
2. To make the scrambled egg whites, heat a non-stick greased skillet and pour the egg whites into it. Let it cook without stirring until you see the edges set. Once set, stir the eggs gently using a spatula to form large curd-like lumps. Remove from heat and set aside.
3. Take a large microwave-safe bowl and pour the beaten egg into it, add the scrambled egg whites, top it with the cheese and place the sliced sausage on top.
4. Microwave for 1.5 minutes on high and transfer to a plate.
5. Serve immediately and enjoy!

Oat Bran Galette - Pancake

Servings: 1

Type: Breakfast

Ingredients:

- 1 1/2 tablespoons oat bran
- 1 full egg or 1 beaten egg white
- 1 1/2 tablespoons cream cheese (non-fat)
- Pinch of cinnamon
- Olive oil, for greasing

Method:

1. Take a medium-sized bowl and place the oat bran in it.
2. Crack the egg and beat it well then pour the beaten egg white into the oat bran bowl
3. Mix them thoroughly until the eggs and oat bran are combined thoroughly
4. Grease the non-stick frying pan with few drops of olive oil and heat it on medium-high
5. Pour the oat-egg mixture into the hot pan and let it cook for 3 minutes. Flip it and continue to cook for 3 more minutes.
6. Transfer to a plate and serve immediately. Enjoy!

Egg Chicken Cheese Bake

Servings: 4

Type: Breakfast or Lunch

Ingredients:

- 2 cups chicken thighs or breasts (cooked and shredded)
- 3 large eggs (beaten)
- 1/2 cup ricotta cheese
- 3 ounces skim mozzarella (shredded)
- 2 tablespoons pimentos
- 1 cup sharp cheddar (shredded)
- 1 tablespoon dried mixed herbs
- 1 cup cottage cheese (non-fat)
- Nonstick cooking spray

Method:

1. Preheat oven to 325 degrees Fahrenheit.
2. Grease a casserole dish with the nonstick cooking spray and set it aside
3. Take a large bowl and combine the shredded cooked chicken and beaten eggs in it
4. Add the pimentos to the bowl. Mix them together until the contents are incorporated well.
5. Add the cottage cheese, cheddar, mozzarella, and ricotta cheese to the mixture.
6. Mix them thoroughly until combined.
7. Transfer the mixed cheese egg-chicken to the greased casserole.
8. Sprinkle the herbs on the top.
9. Bake for 15 minutes until the eggs are cooked and set.

10. The cheese would have melted and given it a soft mushy texture.
11. Transfer to a plate and serve hot. Enjoy!

Breakfast Bars

Servings: 8 bars

Type: Breakfast

Ingredients:

- 2 cups oat bran
- 1/2 cup Egg Beaters (or 2 freshly beaten eggs)
- 1 cup plain Greek yogurt (non-fat)
- 2 teaspoons cinnamon (ground)
- 1/2 cup artificial sweetener (Splenda)
- Nonstick Cooking Spray

Method:

1. Preheat the oven to 325 degrees Fahrenheit
2. Grease an 8 x 8 inch baking pan with the nonstick cooking spray and set aside.
3. Combine the oat bran, beaten eggs, yogurt, cinnamon and Splenda in a large bowl.
4. Mix well until the contents are incorporated nicely.
5. Pour the mixed batter into the baking dish and bake for 45 minutes.
6. Remove from the oven and let it cool completely.
7. Cut it into eight pieces evenly and transfer to a plate.
8. Serve immediately and enjoy!

Meat Loaf

Servings: 12

Type: Breakfast or Lunch

Ingredients:

- 2 1/4 pounds lean beef (minced)
- 1 tablespoon mixed herbs
- 4 tablespoons yogurt (non-fat)
- 2 beaten eggs
- 2 hard-boiled eggs (sliced)
- Salt and pepper, to taste.
- Nonstick cooking spray

Method:

1. Preheat the oven to 350 degrees Fahrenheit.
2. Take a large bowl and place the minced lean beef in it
3. Add the yogurt, beaten eggs, salt, mixed herbs and pepper to the bowl.
4. Mix the contents slowly and carefully until they are incorporated well
5. Grease a loaf pan and add half of the mixture into it.
6. Place the sliced hardboiled eggs neatly in a row over the mixture.
7. Add the remaining mixture (don't fill the loaf pan until the edge as it will rise upwards while baking)
8. Bake for 45 to 60 minutes until the mixture is set.
9. Let it cool for 5 to 10 minutes before slicing.
10. Serve hot or cold and enjoy!

Portuguese Piri Piri Chicken

Servings: 4

Type: Lunch

Ingredients:

- 4 chicken breast fillets (skinless) or 8 chicken drumsticks (skinless)
- 1/4 cup cider vinegar
- 2 teaspoons chilies (crushed)
- 2 finely chopped garlic cloves
- 1 teaspoon paprika
- Salt and black pepper, to taste
- 1 teaspoon oregano
- Juice of half lime (optional)

Method:
1. Take a large bowl and place the chicken in it.
2. Pour the vinegar onto the chicken and add the crushed chilies, garlic, paprika, oregano, salt, and black pepper.
3. Mix them well and marinate it overnight or for a maximum of four hours in the refrigerator.
4. Preheat the broiler in the oven
5. Cook the marinated chicken 6 to 8 inches from the broiler for about 10 to 15 minutes.
6. Turn over to the other side and continue to grill for another 15 minutes
7. Remove from the oven and place it on a bowl.
8. Squeeze the juice of half the lime over the chicken.
9. Serve hot and enjoy!

Chicken Tandoori

Servings: 4

Type: Lunch

Ingredients:

- 6 chicken breast fillets
- 1 teaspoon minced ginger
- 5 tablespoons Greek yogurt (non-fat)
- 3 minced garlic cloves
- 2 teaspoons tandoori spice mix
- Salt and pepper, to taste
- 2 minced chilies
- Nonstick cooking spray

Method:

1. Place the ginger, yogurt, garlic, spice mix, chilies, salt and pepper in a high-speed blender.
2. Blend on high for 1 minute and transfer the contents to a medium-sized bowl.
3. Add the chicken breast to the blended mixture and immerse it completely in the mixture.
4. Allow it to marinate overnight or at least for four hours in the refrigerator.
5. Preheat the oven to its highest temperature.
6. Grease an oven-safe dish or pan and place the marinated chicken fillets in it.
7. Place it in the oven and let it cook on high heat for 20 to 30 minutes (check often to ensure the meat doesn't get burnt)
8. Turn off the oven and leave it in the hot oven for 3 more minutes for tastier flavor.
9. Transfer to a plate and serve warm. Enjoy!

Dukan Breakfast Casserole

Servings: 8

Type: Breakfast

Ingredients:

- 1 cup beaten egg (1 large egg or 2 medium eggs)
- 1 package breakfast turkey sausage
- 2 cups skim milk
- 1 teaspoon poultry seasoning
- 8 ounces part-skim mozzarella cheese (shredded)
- 4 1/2 cups cubed white bread (low-carb, low-fat – check ingredients)
- 1 teaspoon mustard powder
- Nonstick cooking spray
- Salt, to taste

Method:

1. Heat a medium-sized skillet over medium heat.
2. Crumble the sausage into the hot skillet and cook until it is browned
3. Add the poultry seasoning and mix well. Set aside.
4. Grease a 9x13 casserole dish with a cooking spray and set aside.
5. Place the browned sausage in a large bowl.
6. Slightly toast the cubed white bread and add it to the sausage in the bowl.
7. Add the salt, mustard powder, and shredded cheese to the bread-sausage content in the bowl. Mix well and set aside.
8. Combine the beaten eggs and skim milk in a small bowl. Using a hand immersion blender, blend the contents well.

9. Pour the blended egg-milk mixture over the bread-sausage mixture and stir them well until they are combined.
10. Pour this mixture into the greased casserole and spread it evenly. Cover with an aluminum foil and let it refrigerate overnight or for minimum 8 hours.
11. Preheat the oven to 350 degrees Fahrenheit and bake the refrigerated mixture for 45 minutes without removing the foil.
12. Reduce the temperature to 325 degrees Fahrenheit and bake for another 20 minutes until the contents are set.
13. Remove from the oven and let it cool for 5 minutes.
14. Transfer to a plate and serve hot. Enjoy!

Ducan Toast

Servings: 2

Type: Breakfast

Ingredients:

- 2 tablespoons oat bran
- 1 egg
- 1/2 teaspoon baking powder
- 3 1/2 ounces cheese (fat-free)
- 1/2 teaspoon Italian herbs
- Salt and pepper, to taste

For the filling
- 1 light cheese slice
- 1 or 2 baked ham turkey slices

Method:
1. Preheat oven to 350 degrees Fahrenheit
2. Take a medium-sized bowl and crack the egg into it
3. Add the oat bran, baking powder, cheese, Italian herbs, salt and pepper into the bowl.
4. Beat the mixture together until it is completely incorporated and blended well.
5. Line a baking sheet with parchment paper and pour the mixture onto it.
6. Spread it evenly and bake it for 20 minutes until the browning begins
7. Once it browns, remove it from the oven and stuff it with turkey and cheese slices.
8. Close and cover the mixture again. Slice it into two parts and heat it in the grill until it is crisp but soft.
9. Remove from the grill and let it sit for 2 to 4 minutes.
10. Transfer to a plate and serve immediately. Enjoy!

Chicken Burger

Servings: 4

Type: Lunch

Ingredients:

- 1 pound ground chicken
- 3 tablespoons flat leaf Italian parsley (chopped)
- 1 onion (finely chopped) or 1 teaspoon onion powder
- 2 minced garlic cloves
- Mayonnaise Dukan (for garnishing)
- 1 egg (nicely beaten)
- 2 teaspoon Italian seasoning
- Dukan bread slices (as you desire)
- Salt and pepper (freshly ground), to taste

Method:

1. Take a large bowl and place the ground chicken in it.
2. Add the chopped parsley, onion powder (or chopped onions), garlic, Italian seasoning, salt, and pepper.
3. Mix well with your hand until all the contents blend well
4. Pour the beaten egg and fold the mixture slowly using a spatula or large spoon.
5. Using your hand, mix the meat-egg mixture one last time and wrap it to a big ball.
6. Place this seasoned meatball in an aluminum wrap and refrigerate for 30 minutes.
7. Divide the mixture into four and make nice big patties.
8. Preheat the grill to medium heat.
9. Grill the burgers for 6 to 8 minutes approximately on one side.

10. Flip to the other side and grill for 6 more minutes until it is cooked through and browned.
11. Take a slice of Dukan bread, spread some mayonnaise, place the burger and top it with another bread slice.
12. Serve immediately and enjoy (if you are in the cruise phase, you can add some lettuce leaves, sliced tomatoes, and cucumbers to the burger. Relish!)

Egg White Frittata

Servings: 2

Type: Breakfast

Ingredients:

- 5 egg whites (beaten)
- 3 1/2 ounces turkey ham
- 1/2 medium onion (diced)
- 2 tablespoons cheese (fat-free)
- 1/4 teaspoon oregano (dried)
- 1/4 teaspoon salt
- Dash pepper, to taste
- Nonstick cooking spray

Method:

1. Preheat the oven to 325 degrees Fahrenheit
2. Grease an ovenproof skillet with nonstick cooking spray and heat it over medium-high heat
3. Add the onions to the hot skillet and sauté until soft and translucent.
4. Add the turkey ham, oregano, salt and paper to the onions in the skillet.
5. Continue to sauté until the contents are cooked to a soft and tender texture.
6. Pour the foamy beaten egg whites over the contents in the skillet.
7. Reduce the heat to medium-low heat and cook for 3 minutes until the egg is slightly set and gets puffed.
8. Remove from heat and let it sit for a minute or two.
9. Bake this for 15 minutes until the egg whites are set and remove from the oven.

10. Transfer to a plate or just invert the skillet over the plate.
11. Slice it into four wedges and serve immediately. Enjoy!

Oopsie Bread

Servings: 6

Type: Breakfast

Ingredients:

- 3 eggs
- 1/8 teaspoon cream of tartar
- 3 ounces cream cheese (Fat-free)
- Nonstick cooking spray

Method:

1. Take a bowl and crack the eggs. Separate the egg whites and the yolks.
2. Add the cream cheese to the egg yolks. Mix the contents well using a mixer or blender.
3. In another bowl, combine the egg whites and cream of tartar. Whip the contents until stiff (in case you are using the same mixer, mix the egg whites fast and then go ahead with the yolk mixture)
4. Add the egg yolk mixture to the egg white mixture by slowly folding the yolk mixture using a spatula.
5. You will need to do it carefully else you might break down the whites.
6. Preheat the oven to 300 degrees Fahrenheit
7. Grease the cookie sheet with a nonstick cooking spray.
8. Spoon the mixture onto the greased cookie sheet and make 6 mounds.
9. Using the back of the spoon, flatten each mound slightly and slowly
10. Bake them for 30 minutes until the contents set – they should not get crumbly but a bit soft

11. Let it sit for a few minutes before you move it to a rack and allow it to cool completely.
12. Transfer to an open container and let it rest for some more time until the moisture goes off.
13. Serve warm and enjoy! You can also freeze it and use!

(Note: You can add a bit of stevia to the yolk mixture if you want your bread to be sweet, or you can add dill / dry mustard / other seasonings to the yolk mixture if you want the bread to be a savory)

Easy Meat Loaf

Servings: 8

Type: Dinner

Ingredients:

- 17 ounces minced lean meat
- 1 egg (beaten)
- 1/4 cup oat bran
- 1 chopped onions
- 2 tablespoons Dijon mustard
- 4 tablespoons diet ketchup (sugar-free)

Method:

1. Preheat the oven to 375 degrees Fahrenheit
2. Take a large bowl and place the minced lean meat
3. Pour the beaten egg over the meat and mix well until combined
4. Add the oat bran and onions to the meat-egg mixture.
5. Combine together all the contents until blended completely. Set aside.
6. Mix together the Dijon mustard and 2 tablespoons of diet ketchup in a small bowl.
7. Line a loaf pan with parchment paper and spread the meat-egg mixture onto it evenly.
8. Brush the ketchup-mustard mixture over the meatloaf generously.
9. Bake for 1 hour and 15 minutes until the meat cooks and browns
10. Let it cool for sometime before you slice it.
11. Transfer the slices to a plate and serve warm with remaining 2 tablespoons ketchup. Enjoy!

Rosemary and Garlic Chicken

Servings: 2

Type: Dinner

Ingredients:

- 2 skinless chicken breasts (diced)
- Rosemary, to taste
- 3 minced garlic cloves (fresh)
- 2 tablespoons Dijon mustard
- 1 onion (diced)
- 1/8 cup lemon juice
- Nonstick cooking spray
- 1/2 cup water
- Salt and pepper, to taste

Method:

1. Grease a frying pan with nonstick cooking spray and heat it.
2. Add the garlic to the hot pan and roast it until the raw flavors go
3. Add the rosemary to the roasted garlic and continue to cook as you stir the contents
4. Add the diced chicken to the pan and pour 1/2 cup water over it.
5. Add the Dijon, salt, pepper and lemon juice to the chicken in the pan
6. Stir the contents until combined.
7. Cover the pan and let it cook until the chicken is soft and tender.
8. Once the chicken is cooked, add the diced onion to it and stir well.

9. Continue to cook until the onions turn translucent and soft.
10. Transfer to a plate and serve hot. Enjoy!

Scrambled Eggs with Chicken, Cream Cheese, and Chives

Servings: 1

Type: Dinner

Ingredients:

- 2 egg whites
- 1 tablespoon fat-free cream cheese
- 1 egg
- 1 tablespoon chives
- 1 shredded and cooked chicken breast
- Nonstick cooking spray
- Salt and pepper, to taste

Method:

1. Crack the egg in a large bowl and add the 2 egg whites into it.
2. Beat it well until combined
3. Add the cream cheese and chives to the egg mixture.
4. Combine it well until the contents blend completely.
5. Grease a large skillet with the nonstick cooking spray and heat it over medium heat
6. Add the shredded cooked chicken and sauté until it turns brown slightly (roasted)
7. Pour the egg-cheese mixture over the chicken and season it with salt and pepper.
8. Scramble the egg slowly and continue to stir until the eggs are completely cooked.
9. You can add more pepper if you like. Transfer to a plate and serve warm. Enjoy!

Egg Drop Soup

Servings: 4

Type: Dinner

Ingredients:

- 2 eggs
- 4 cups low fat chicken broth
- 1 egg yolks
- 2 tablespoons chopped chives
- 1/8 teaspoon ginger powder
- Salt, to taste

Method:

1. Heat a large saucepan over medium heat.
2. Pour the chicken broth into the hot pan
3. Add the ginger powder, chives, and salt to the broth. Bring the mixture to a rolling boil.
4. Crack the eggs in a small bowl and add the egg yolks to it. Use a fork to whisk together the egg yolk and the cracked egg until well blended
5. Now, get to the boiling broth mixture and drizzle the egg little by little with the fork to the boiling mixture
6. Since the liquid is boiling, the egg droppings will get cooked immediately
7. Continue to stir the soup after all the eggs have been dropped.
8. Once you get the desired consistency, turn off the heat and transfer to a bowl.
9. Serve hot and enjoy!

Roast Beef and Mayo

Servings: 2

Type: Dinner

Ingredients:

- 10 ounces Beef Fillet
- 1 Egg yolk
- 3 tablespoons fat-free Greek yogurt
- 1 tablespoon rosemary (dried and ground)
- 1 tablespoon dried thyme
- 1 tablespoon Dijon mustard
- 1 tablespoon chives (chopped)
- Salt and Pepper, to taste
- Olive oil, for greasing

Method:

1. Carefully tie the beef fillet into a round shape.
2. Season it with salt, thyme, and rosemary. Set aside
3. Preheat the oven to 390 degrees Fahrenheit
4. Grease a large skillet with few drops of olive oil and heat it over medium-high heat
5. Place the seasoned beef fillet on the hot pan and fry all its sides for a minute or two.
6. Place the fried fillet on a baking tray and allow it to cook in the oven for 20 to 25 minutes
7. Combine the egg yolk and mustard in a mixing bowl. Add some salt and pepper to the egg-mustard mixture and stir well.
8. Now add the yogurt and chopped chives to the egg mixture.
9. Stir again until the contents are well incorporated.
10. Refrigerate the prepared mayonnaise for few minutes.

11. Remove the beef from the oven and cover it with an aluminum foil for 5 minutes
12. Slice the cooked beef into easy-to-bite pieces and transfer to a plate.
13. Serve immediately and enjoy with the chive mayonnaise.

Butterflied Chicken Breast with Rosemary

Servings: 1

Type: Dinner

Ingredients:

- 1 chicken breast (skinless, boneless, butterflied)
- 2 teaspoons rosemary needles (coarsely chopped)
- 1/2 teaspoon salt
- 1 tablespoon lemon juice
- 1/4 teaspoon black pepper
- Nonstick cooking spray

For brining the chicken breast
- Kosher salt, as required
- 1 cup warm water

Method:

1. Pour a cup of warm water in a large bowl.
2. Add kosher salt to the water and stir well until the salt is dissolved completely
3. Add the butterflied chicken breast to the salt water and let it sit for 10 minutes to brine
4. Remove from the water and season the meat by rubbing it with pepper and rosemary
5. Heat a greased nonstick pan over high heat until it starts smoking.
6. Place the seasoned chicken in the hot pan and fry it until the chicken is completely cooked
7. Alternate between the sides while frying for every half to one minute until the breast is cooked on all side.
8. Squeeze over the lemon juice and transfer to a plate.
9. Serve immediately and enjoy!

Salmon with Mustard and Dill Sauce

Servings: 2 - 4

Type: Dinner

Ingredients:

- 4 salmon fillets
- 1 tablespoon classic mustard
- 1 finely chopped dill
- 6 tablespoons cottage cheese (non-fat)
- Salt and Pepper, to taste
- 2 chopped green onions
- Nonstick cooking spray

Method:

1. Freeze the salmon fillets for 5 to 8 minutes and then cut them into fine strips
2. Grease a nonstick frying pan with cooking spray and heat it over medium heat
3. Cook the salmon strips in the hot pan on both sides (a minute for each side) and transfer them into a dish
4. Add the onions to the same skillet and cook until soft and tender.
5. Add the mustard and cheese to the skillet. Continue to cook for a minute until the sauce thickens
6. Now place the cooked salmon strips over the sauce and coat it well.
7. Add salt, dill, and pepper to the coated strips. Turn off the heat and transfer to a plate
8. Serve warm and enjoy!

Chapter Six: Cruise Phase Recipes

Cauliflower Broccoli Cheese Bake

Servings: 6

Type: Breakfast or Lunch

Ingredients:

- 2 cups largely chopped cauliflower
- 3 cups largely chopped broccoli
- 1/2 cup ricotta cheese
- 1/2 yellow bell pepper (chopped)
- 3 ounces skim mozzarella (shredded)
- 2 tablespoons pimentos
- 1 cup sharp cheddar (shredded)
- 1 cup cottage cheese (non-fat)
- Nonstick cooking spray

Method:

1. Preheat oven to 325 degrees Fahrenheit.
2. Grease a casserole dish with the nonstick cooking spray and set it aside
3. Take a large bowl and combine the chopped broccoli and cauliflower in it
4. Add the bell pepper and pimentos to the bowl. Mix them together.
5. Add the cottage cheese, cheddar, mozzarella, and ricotta cheese to the vegetables.
6. Mix them thoroughly until combined.
7. Transfer the mixed cheese vegetables to the greased casserole.
8. Bake for 15 minutes until the vegetables are cooked but crispy on the outside.
9. The cheese would have melted and given it a soft mushy texture.
10. Transfer to a plate and serve hot. Enjoy!

Cabbage Chili

Servings: 1

Type: Lunch

Ingredients:

- 3 1/2 ounces cabbage (shredded or finely chopped)
- 3 1/2 ounces chicken breast or lean ground beef
- 2 garlic cloves
- 3 1/2 ounces ripe tomato
- 1 teaspoon thyme (ground)
- 2 cups water
- 1 teaspoon cumin (ground)
- 1 teaspoon oregano
- 1 teaspoon chili powder
- Salt and pepper, to taste

Method:

1. Heat a large pot over medium-high heat and place the meat in it.
2. Pour 2 cups of water over the meat and add the garlic cloves to it.
3. Add the thyme, cumin, oregano, chili powder, salt and pepper to the meat in the pot.
4. Stir well and let it come to boil.
5. When the water is too hot, add the chopped cabbage and let it cook until the vegetable becomes soft and tender
6. Now add the tomato to the pot and continue to cook.
7. The tomato will be softer if you cook for a longer time.
8. Reduce the heat and cover the pot.
9. Simmer for 15 to 20 minutes until the meat and vegetables are completely cooked.

10. Turn off the heat once the liquid is completely gone and transfer to a plate.
11. Serve warm and enjoy!

Dukan Salmon and Broccoli Tabbouleh

Servings: 1

Type: Dinner

Ingredients:

- 1 salmon fillet
- 1/3 cup broccoli florets
- 2 trimmed and sliced spring onions
- Small handful chopped parsley
- 2 tablespoons oat bran
- Small handful chopped mint,
- Grated zest of 1/2 lime
- Salt and pepper, to taste

Method:

1. Take a medium-sized bowl and place the oat bran in it.
2. Pour two tablespoons of boiling water over the oat bran and let it stand for 10 minutes
3. Take another bowl and pour boiling water into it. Immerse the broccoli florets in the water and let it sit for 5 to 10 minutes.
4. Remove from the hot water and plunge them into ice-cold water or refresh under cold running water
5. Go back to the oat bran and fluff it with a fork.
6. Add the parsley, mint, spring onions, blanched broccoli, and lime zest to the fluffed oat bran.
7. Mix it well and season with salt and pepper. Your Tabbouleh is ready. Set aside
8. Grill the salmon fillet in the oven and transfer to a plate.

9. Flake the grilled fish a bit and mix it with prepared Tabbouleh.
10. Serve warm and enjoy!

Fish and Cauliflower Gratin

Servings: 4

Type: Lunch

Ingredients:

- 7 ounces king prawns (cooked and peeled)
- 6 ounces trimmed cauliflower
- 10 ounces white fish fillet or skinless cod (preferably sustainably caught)
- 1 quartered small onion
- 10 ounces smoked haddock (skinless)
- 1 tablespoon finely grated Parmesan cheese
- 2 cups skimmed milk
- 3 tablespoons corn flour
- 2 tablespoons Dukan breadcrumbs (fresh)
- 2 small bay leaves

Method:

1. Heat a frying pan over medium heat.
2. Place the onion in the hot pan and fry it a few seconds until it browns a bit
3. Add the fish (cod and haddock) and bay leaf to the onions in the pan.
4. Pour the milk over the contents and simmer.
5. Cover the pan and let it cook for 2 to 4 minutes
6. Turn off the heat and let it sit for 10 minutes (let the pan be covered)
7. Preheat the oven to 392 degrees Fahrenheit.
8. Slice the trimmed cauliflower into 1.5-inch pieces. Blanch the, rinse and drain thoroughly.
9. Place the drained cauliflower in a large bowl and add 1-tablespoon breadcrumbs to it.

10. Add the grated Parmesan cheese and mix the contents thoroughly.
11. Meanwhile, drain the fish into a bowl and pour the milk back into the frying pan.
12. Mix 3 tablespoons of water with corn flour in a small bowl.
13. Add this to the milk in the frying pan, reduce the heat and whisk carefully until you can a thick consistency.
14. Discard the bay leaf and onion from the cooked fish.
15. Add the fish back to the sauce in the pan and add the cheese cauliflower to it.
16. Now, add the cooked prawn and mix the contents of the pan thoroughly.
17. Transfer this mixture to an ovenproof dish and sprinkle the remaining breadcrumbs over it.
18. Bake this for 25 minutes until golden brown.
19. Let it cool for 5 minutes and transfer to a serving plate.
20. Serve warm and enjoy!

Baked Monkfish and Tomato Loaf

Servings: 6

Type: Dinner

Ingredients:

- 1 pound fresh monkfish
- 1/4 cup tomato sauce
- 1 tablespoon persillade OR (1/2 tablespoon chopped parsley + 1/2 tablespoon minced garlic)
- 3 eggs
- One head of lettuce (rinsed)
- 1 chicken stock cube
- Salt and pepper, to taste
- Balsamic vinegar
- Olive oil, for greasing

Method:

1. Boil a cup of water in a saucepan and dissolve the chicken stock cube in it
2. Add the monkfish to the boiled chicken stock water and let it cook for 15 minutes
3. Preheat the oven to 350 degrees Fahrenheit
4. Remove the cooked fish from the chicken stock water and drain it using a strainer.
5. Slice the fish into small cubes and set it aside
6. Take a small bowl and crack the eggs into it. Add the tomato sauce to the cracked eggs and mix together until well blended.
7. Season it with salt and pepper. Mix again.
8. Add the persillade (OR parsley + garlic mixture) to the egg-tomato mixture and mix it well until the contents are incorporated well enough.

9. Grease a loaf pan with few drops of olive oil and spread the fish cubes in the bottom.
10. Pour the egg mixture evenly over the top of the lined fish cubes in the loaf pan.
11. Bake for 30 minutes until the fish and egg get cooked completely.
12. In case the contents browns too soon, cover the pan with aluminum foil for the remaining cooking time and continue
13. Remove from the oven and let it sit for 15 minutes.
14. Take off the foil and carefully remove the baked fish-egg from the loaf pan.
15. You can run a butter knife along the edges of the pan to extricate from the sides of the pan.
16. Invert it onto a plate and set aside
17. Tear the lettuce leaves into easy-to-bite pieces and divide them among six plates.
18. Slice the loaf evenly and place one each over the lettuce.
19. Sprinkle a dash of balsamic vinegar and serve. Enjoy!

Thai Beef Skewers

Servings: 4

Type: Breakfast

Ingredients:

- 1 pound cubed lean sirloin steak
- 3 finely chopped garlic cloves
- 2 teaspoons red pepper flakes
- 2 teaspoons fresh ginger (minced and peeled)
- 1/2 cup soy sauce
- 2 teaspoons mirin
- 4 teaspoons plain rice vinegar
- 2 teaspoons fish sauce
- 2 teaspoons toasted sesame oil
- Juice of 1 lime
- 1 packet stevia

Method:

1. Take a medium-sized bowl and combine together the garlic cloves, red pepper flakes, ginger, soy sauce, mirin, rice vinegar, fish sauce, sesame oil, lime juice, and stevia.
2. Mix thoroughly until the contents blend well.
3. Place the cubed meat in the mixture and let it marinate overnight in the refrigerator.
4. Take a skewer and thread around 4 to 5 marinated meat cubes in it.
5. Repeat step 5 with the remaining marinated meat chunks with the other skewers.
6. Grill them for about 3 to 4 minutes until completely cooked. Flip around to the other sides and continue until thoroughly grilled.
7. Transfer to a plate and serve immediately. Enjoy!

Steamed Mussels and Clams

Servings: 4

Type: Lunch

Ingredients:

- 1 pound cleaned mussels
- 1 cup chicken broth
- 1 pound cleaned clams
- 1/2 cup parsley (flat leaf)
- 1/2 onion (diced)
- 1 tomato (diced)
- Juice of 1/2 lemon
- Salt, to taste

Method:

1. Take a large pot and pour the chicken broth.
2. Heat the pot over medium-high heat
3. Add the parsley, onion, tomato, and lemon juice to the broth. All the contents will by lying in the bottom of the pot.
4. Reduce the heat to medium-low and bring the contents to simmer.
5. Allow the contents to simmer for around 5 to 10 minutes
6. Now, add the cleaned clams and mussels to the pot. Season it with required salt and cover.
7. Allow the contents to cook for 5 to 10 minutes until the clams and mussels open up
8. Remove from heat and transfer to a bowl.
9. Serve warm and enjoy.

Spinach Quiche

Servings: 4

Type: Breakfast

Ingredients:

- 12 ounces spinach (a bag)
- 3 eggs (large)
- 1/2 cup red peppers (chopped)
- 2 egg whites
- 1 cup cauliflower stems (chopped)
- 2 tablespoons Parmesan cheese
- 1/2 cup onion (chopped)
- 1/2 cup skim milk
- Salt and pepper, to taste
- Nonstick cooking spray

Method:

1. Preheat the oven to 375 degrees Fahrenheit
2. Grease a frying pan with nonstick cooking spray and heat over medium-high heat
3. Add the onion to the hot pan and reduce to medium-low heat.
4. Stir-fry until the onions are soft and tender. Add the cauliflower and red peppers to the sautéed onions
5. Continue to cook for around 8 minutes until the vegetables soften
6. Now, add the spinach to the pan and cover it. Cook for 2 to 3 minutes until the spinach wilts and is completely cooked.
7. Take a medium-sized bowl and crack the eggs into it.
8. Add the egg whites, parmesan cheese, skim milk, salt and pepper to the cracked eggs

9. Mix together until they are thoroughly blended.
10. Add the spinach-cauliflower-bell pepper mixture to this egg-milk mixture. Combine them until the contents are incorporated well.
11. Grease a round baking dish and pour this mixture into it.
12. Bake for 30 minutes until the spinach quiche is cooked completely.
13. Remove from oven and let it cool for a while. Slice them up and transfer to a plate.
14. Serve warm or cold and enjoy!

Spicy Lemon Roasted Chicken

Servings: 4-6

Type: Lunch

Ingredients:

- 6 pound chicken (cleaned)
- 1 large lemon, halved
- 1 1/2 teaspoon ground cumin
- 1/2 teaspoon ground black pepper
- 1 teaspoon onion powder
- 1 teaspoon paprika
- 1/2 teaspoon chili powder
- 1 teaspoon garlic powder
- 1 tablespoon olive oil
- 1/2 teaspoon salt

Method:

1. Preheat the oven to 375 degrees Fahrenheit
2. Place the chicken in a plate and squeeze the lemon juice over it.
3. Rub the lemon on the chicken and place the halves in the cavity. Set aside.
4. Combine together the olive oil, garlic powder, chili powder, paprika, onion powder, black pepper, cumin, and salt in a small bowl.
5. Rub this spice mixture all over the chicken until it is completely coated with the seasoning.
6. Place the dressed chicken in a greased baking tray and roast it for 1 hour and 45 minutes.
7. When the meat is completely roasted and cooked, remove from the oven.

8. Let it rest for 15 minutes and transfer to a serving plate.
9. Serve hot or warm and enjoy!

Prosciutto Wrapped Asparagus with Egg

Servings: 4

Type: Dinner or Breakfast

Ingredients:

- 1 pound asparagus (fresh)
- 4 eggs
- 4 pieces prosciutto, bacon or ham
- Salt and pepper, to taste
- Nonstick cooking spray
- Mixed herbs, as desired (optional)

Method:

1. Preheat oven to 400 degrees Fahrenheit
2. Wash and trim the asparagus, season it with pepper and salt as per your taste.
3. Divide the asparagus among 4 plates evenly and wrap each bundle with a piece of ham or prosciutto or bacon.
4. Grease a baking tray with nonstick cooking spray and place the meat-wrapped asparagus on it.
5. Bake for 20 minutes until the meat and asparagus are completely cooked
6. Meanwhile, heat a nonstick skillet over medium-high heat and crack one egg on the hot skillet. Season it with salt and pepper (optional: you can add mixed herbs if you like).
7. Once the omelet is ready, serve it over one bundle of meat-wrapped asparagus.
8. Repeat step 6 and 7 for the remaining 3 eggs. Serve warm and enjoy!

Rosemary Grilled Chicken

Servings: 4

Type: Lunch

Ingredients:

- 2 tablespoons minced fresh rosemary
- 4 boneless and skinless chicken breasts (1 piece can be around 6 ounces)
- 6 minced garlic cloves
- 1 teaspoon smoked paprika
- 1/8 teaspoon black pepper
- 1/4 cup lemon juice
- 2 tablespoons olive oil
- 1/4 teaspoon salt

Method:

1. Combine together rosemary, garlic, paprika, black pepper, lemon juice, olive oil and salt in a large bowl.
2. Coat the chicken with the mixture and place it in the bowl. Let it marinate for 4 hours or overnight in the refrigerator.
3. Preheat the grill in the oven.
4. Place the chicken in a pan or tray and place it on the grill rack.
5. Let the meat cook for at least 20 minutes (or more depending on the thickness of the breast)
6. Transfer to a plate and serve hot. Enjoy!

Slow Cooker Shredded Beef

Servings: 8

Type: Dinner

Ingredients:

- 2 1/2 pound beef roast (trimmed of all fat)
- 1 cup beef broth
- 1 teaspoon dried oregano
- 1/2 cup apple cider vinegar
- 1 teaspoon garlic powder
- 1 teaspoon black pepper (freshly ground)
- 1 teaspoon onion powder
- 1 teaspoon chili powder
- 1 teaspoon cumin
- 2 teaspoon smoked paprika
- Kosher salt, to taste

Method:

1. Take a small bowl and combine together the dried oregano, garlic powder, black pepper, onion powder, chili powder, cumin, paprika, and salt and apple cider vinegar.
2. Mix them well until the flavors are incorporated.
3. Coat the meat with the spice mixture thoroughly.
4. Pour the beef broth on a slow cooker and add the coated beef to it.
5. Cover and cook on low for 8 hours until the meat is thoroughly cooked.
6. Transfer to a plate and shred it with a fork.
7. Serve warm and enjoy!

Steamed Cajun Shrimp

Servings: 4

Type: Breakfast

Ingredients:

- 1 pound shrimp (around 26 to 30 pieces)
- 1/2 tablespoon cayenne pepper
- 1 tablespoon celery salt
- 1/2 teaspoon ginger (ground)
- 1/2 tablespoon paprika
- 1/2 tablespoon garlic powder
- 1 tablespoon seasoning (Italian or Old Bay)
- 1/2 tablespoon salt
- 1 cup water
- Juice of 1 lemon

Method:

1. Take a medium-sized pot and pour one cup of water into it.
2. Add the lemon juice along with cayenne pepper, celery salt, ground ginger, paprika, garlic powder, seasoning, and salt.
3. Stir well and bring the liquid to boil over medium-high heat.
4. Add the shrimps when the liquid is boiling and reduce the heat to medium-low.
5. Let it simmer while you cover the pot.
6. Cook the shrimp for 6 minutes until the fish becomes opaque (it will turn pink).
7. When the shrimp is thoroughly cooked, transfer to a plate and serve cold or hot.

8. You can also add boiled vegetables or starchy ones depending on your Dukan Diet phases.

Chive Pancakes

Servings: 1

Type: Breakfast

Ingredients:

- 1 tablespoon chives
- 2 tablespoons oat bran
- 1 egg
- 1 tablespoon powdered milk (non-fat)
- Salt and pepper, to taste
- 1/4 teaspoon baking soda
- Nonstick cooking spray

Method:

1. Take a medium-sized bowl and crack the egg in it.
2. Add the oat bran, powdered milk, salt, pepper, and baking soda into the cracked egg.
3. Whisk together until the contents blend well
4. Add the chives and fold it in gently.
5. Grease a nonstick skillet with cooking spray and spoon in the chive batter.
6. Flatten it a bit and let it cook on medium heat for 4 minutes per side.
7. Flip it over and cook for 4 more minutes.
8. Transfer to a plate and serve hot!
9. Continue steps 5 to 7 with the remaining batter.

Sautéed Mini Mushroom Frittatas

Servings: 12

Type: Breakfast

Ingredients:

- 8 ounces cleaned and sliced cremini mushrooms
- 8 egg whites
- 1 medium yellow onion (thinly sliced)
- 4 whole eggs
- 4 ounces Swiss cheese (reduced fat)
- 1 tablespoon butter (unsalted)
- 1/2 teaspoon Worcestershire
- 1/2 teaspoon fresh thyme leaves (finely chopped)
- 2 tablespoons skim milk
- Salt and pepper, to taste
- Nonstick cooking spray

Method:

1. Preheat the oven to 350 degrees Fahrenheit
2. Melt the butter in a nonstick frying pan over medium-low heat.
3. Add the onions to the melted butter and stir-fry them for 20 to 25 minutes until they turn deep brown and are completely caramelized.
4. Keep stirring to prevent the onion from getting burnt.
5. Add the thyme, salt, and pepper to the cooked onions. Stir for a while until the contents are cooked
6. Transfer the onions and thyme to a different plate
7. Add the mushrooms to the same pan and season it with pepper and salt as desired.
8. Continue to cook for 10 minutes until the mushrooms soften

9. Since there will be butter left over in the pan, the mushrooms won't burn. You can add some cooking spray if required.
10. Add the cooked onions back to the pan and give it a stir.
11. Meanwhile, take a small bowl and whisk together the milk, egg whites, salt, eggs, and Worcestershire.
12. Add the cheese to the whisked mixture and stir well.
13. Grease the 12 muffin cups with cooking spray and divide the mushroom mixture equally between the cups
14. Now, pour the egg mixture over the cups and bake for 15 minutes until completely cooked through
15. Once the frittatas are done, let it sit for 10 minutes.
16. Serve warm or cold and enjoy!

Broccoli Soup

Servings: 8

Type: Dinner

Ingredients:

- 2 1/2 pounds chopped broccoli
- 4 cups chicken broth
- 1 medium chopped onion
- 3 ounces grated cheddar (sharp low-fat)
- 2 minced garlic cloves
- 1 1/2 ounces grated parmesan
- 1 1/2 teaspoon dry mustard powder
- 1/4 teaspoon baking soda
- 1/2 teaspoon Cayenne powder
- Salt and pepper, to taste
- Nonstick cooking spray

Method:

1. Grease a large pot with nonstick cooking spray and heat it over medium heat.
2. Add the broccoli, mustard, onion, cayenne, garlic, and 1 teaspoon salt to the hot greased pot
3. Cook for 5 minutes until the broccoli turns fragrant and the onions are translucent
4. Pour a cup of chicken broth over the contents of the pot and add the baking soda.
5. Reduce the flame and let it simmer for around 20 minutes until the broccoli is tender and soft
6. Pour the remaining broth and continue to simmer the soup.
7. Add the cheddar and Parmesan cheese to the simmering soup.

8. Use an immersion blender and blend carefully while the soup continues to simmer
9. Season it with salt and pepper.
10. Transfer to a serving bowl and enjoy hot!

Eggplant Rollatini

Servings: 4

Type: Dinner

Ingredients:

- 1 large eggplant (sliced)
- 1/2 can diced tomatoes (with Italian seasoning)
- 16 ounces ricotta cheese (fat-free)
- 2 tablespoons Italian seasoning
- 4 ounces mozzarella cheese (fat-free)
- Salt and pepper, to taste
- Nonstick cooking spray

Method:

1. Preheat the oven to 350 degrees Fahrenheit
2. Grease a baking sheet with nonstick cooking spray.
3. Spread the sliced eggplants evenly on the tray
4. Bake for 10 minutes and then to the other side and continue to bake for another 10 minutes until both the sides are slightly browned.
5. The cooking time might vary depending on how thick your slices are
6. Combine together the diced tomatoes, ricotta, Italian seasoning, mozzarella, salt and pepper in a large bowl.
7. Mix thoroughly until the flavors blend well.
8. Take around 2 tablespoons of this mixture and place on the eggplant slice. Roll the slices and keep them on the same baking tray.
9. Continue step 8 with the remaining eggplant slices and if you have the cheese tomato mixture remaining, pour it over the rollatini

10. Bake this for 15 minutes until the cheese begins to melt and bubble on all the sides.
11. Transfer to a plate and serve hot! Enjoy!

Chicken Lettuce Wraps

Servings: 4

Type: Dinner

Ingredients:

- 1 pound ground chicken (lean)
- Butter lettuce for cups
- 8 ounces chopped water chestnuts
- 8 chopped scallions
- 1/2 red pepper (chopped)
- 1/4 cup cilantro
- 1 tablespoon ginger (grated)
- 1/4 cup soy sauce
- 2 tablespoons chili paste
- 1 garlic clove
- 1 tablespoon water

Method:

1. Heat a large nonstick skillet over medium-high heat.
2. Add the ground chicken to the hot skillet and brown the meat until all the excess fat oozes out.
3. Discard the fat and place the chicken back into the skillet.
4. Add water chestnuts, scallions, red pepper, soy sauce, chili paste, garlic and water to the chicken in the skillet
5. Mix well and cook for 7 minutes until the red pepper softens.
6. Now, add the cilantro and stir the contents one last time.
7. Transfer the contents into the lettuce cups and serve warm
8. You can also use soy sauce or Asian chili paste as dipping sauces (optional)

Chapter Seven: Consolidation Phase Recipes

Chicken in a Spicy Sauce

Servings: 2

Type: Lunch

Ingredients:

- 4 chicken legs
- 8 teaspoons sour cream (fat-free)
- 1 tablespoon capers
- 1 chopped shallot
- 1 cup tolerated white wine
- 1 tablespoon whole grain mustard
- 1 teaspoon paprika
- Olive oil, for greasing
- Salt and pepper, to taste

Method:

1. Grease the casserole dish (stovetop) with few drops of olive oil and place it over medium heat
2. Add the chicken legs to the hot casserole dish and brown the meat.
3. Add the shallots and continue to cook until the shallots are slightly browned.
4. Add the white wine when the chicken begins to brown. Season it with salt and pepper.
5. Mix the contents until the flavors are incorporated
6. Reduce the heat to low and let it cook for 45 minutes to one hour.
7. The saucy liquid would have reduced by now.
8. Slowly add the sour cream, paprika, capers, and mustard while you continue to stir the contents.
9. Let it simmer for 2 to 3 minutes. Transfer to a plate.
10. Serve hot and enjoy!

Smoked Haddock Scotch Eggs with Asparagus

Servings: 4-6

Type: Breakfast or dinner

Ingredients:

- 14 ounces broccoli (cut into chunks)
- 16 quail eggs
- 14 ounces haddock (skinned and smoked), cut into large chunks
- 2 beaten eggs
- 1/2 cup Dukan breadcrumbs
- 2 tablespoons skimmed milk
- 1/4 cup corn flour
- Olive oil (few drops), for frying
- Asparagus (a small bundle)

For the watercress mayonnaise
- 3 1/2 ounces watercress
- 5 fluid ounces Dukan mayonnaise
- 1 tablespoon lemon juice

Method:
1. Pour water in a large pan and immerse the broccoli in it. Bring it to boil.
2. Add the hammock to the pan and add the quail eggs after a while
3. Allow the eggs to cook for precisely 2 minutes and then remove them from the pan.
4. Cool the cooked eggs in cold running water and keep them aside.

5. Continue to cook the haddock and broccoli until the fish flakes and the vegetable turns soft and tender.
6. Drain the broccoli and fish and place them in a bowl.
7. Add milk to it and mash it to a thick consistency. Set it aside and allow it to cool
8. Now, peel the eggs and keep it ready.
9. When the mashed broccoli-fish has completely cooled down, take one or two spoons of the mashed mix and mold them carefully around the eggs.
10. The eggs should be completely encased with the mash.
11. Place the corn flour on a plate, the beaten eggs in a small bowl and breadcrumbs in another plate.
12. Roll the coated eggs in corn flour first, then in the beaten eggs and finally in the breadcrumbs.
13. Continue steps 9 to 12 with the remaining eggs and set them aside.
14. Refrigerate for an hour for them to firm up.
15. To prepare the watercress mayonnaise, pulse the watercress along with lemon juice until coarse or granular (you can use a food processor).
16. Add the Dukan mayonnaise to the blitzed watercress and set aside.
17. Blanch the cleaned asparagus for 4 to 5 minutes and drain under cold water (you can do this a day before you are preparing this recipe)
18. Heat few drops of olive oil in a frying pan over medium heat.
19. Place the eggs on the hot pan and fry the set eggs until they are crispy from all sides.
20. Place the fried eggs on paper towels to drain the oil.
21. Serve the eggs with watercress mayonnaise and asparagus.
22. Enjoy warm or cold.

Tomato Clafoutis

Servings: 6

Type: Breakfast

Ingredients:

- Cherry tomatoes (one package)
- 1 1/2 cups skimmed milk
- 6 Eggs
- 6 teaspoon cornflour
- 1 1/2 cups sour cream (fat-free)
- Olive oil, few drops for frying
- Pinch of Splenda
- Salt and pepper, to taste

Method:

1. Heat a frying pan and add a few drops of olive oil.
2. Add the tomatoes to the hot pan and sauté for 5 minutes.
3. Add a pinch of Splenda or a bit more as cherry tomatoes tend to get bitter as you cook them.
4. Preheat the oven to 350 degrees Fahrenheit
5. Grease an ovenproof cooking bowl or dish and set aside
6. Take a small bowl and crack the eggs into it. Add the milk, corn flour, sour cream, salt and pepper to the cracked eggs
7. Mix them well until the contents are thoroughly blended.
8. Place the cooked tomatoes in the ovenproof dish and pour the egg cream mixture over it.
9. Bake for 20 minutes until the egg is cooked and the cream melts.
10. Transfer to a plate and serve hot or warm. Enjoy!

King Prawn Lunch Delight

Servings: 2

Type: Lunch

Ingredients:

- 3 ounces prawns
- 3 cups broccoli
- 1 teaspoon scallions
- 8 cherry tomatoes
- 3 minced garlic cloves
- 1 teaspoon Sichuan pepper
- 1 teaspoon Red chili
- 2 tablespoons Lemon juice
- 1 teaspoon Rosemary
- 2 tablespoons Olive Oil
- 1 teaspoon Basil
- Salt & Pepper, to taste

Method:

1. Place the prawns in a colander and rinse them under running water. Clean well and place them on paper towels. Let them dry or pat them dry.
2. Take a small bowl and mix together half of the minced garlic, lemon juice, rosemary, basil, salt, and pepper.
3. Marinate the cleaned prawns in this spice mixture for about 30 minutes in the refrigerator.
4. Meanwhile, chop the broccoli and boil it in salted water in a soup pot. (3 cups of water + pinch of salt). Continue to cook until the broccoli becomes soft.
5. Now, drain the broccoli and immediately run it under cold water. Place it in a colander and let it drain.

6. Heat a non-stick pan and cook the marinated prawns for 8 to 10 minutes until soft and tender. Leave it aside.
7. Heat the olive oil in another small saucepan over medium-high heat for 20 to 30 seconds.
8. Add the Sichuan pepper and red chili pepper to the hot oil in the pan. Reduce the heat to low and cook for 45 seconds to one minute until the peppers turn black or dark brown. Turn off the heat.
9. Take a large mixing bowl and place the drained broccoli in it. Season it with salt and the remaining minced garlic. Mix well.
10. Pour the hot pepper oil over the broccoli and toss it for a while (you can discard the peppers if you want and only pour the oil)
11. Add the cooked prawns to the broccoli in the bowl and stir it once.
12. Transfer to a plate and decorate with the tomatoes. Serve warm and enjoy!

Chinese Style Tomato Egg Stir Fry

Servings: 2

Type: Breakfast

Ingredients:

- 2 medium tomatoes (diced)
- 1 egg (beaten)
- 1 tablespoon chopped green onions with tops
- 2 egg whites (beaten)
- 2 tablespoons low-sodium soy sauce
- 1 teaspoon Stevia
- Salt & Pepper, to taste
- Olive oil, for greasing

Method:

1. Grease a frying pan with few drops of olive oil and heat it over medium-high heat
2. Pour the beaten egg and egg whites into the hot pan and scramble it. No overcooking, please!
3. Transfer the scrambled egg back to the bowl.
4. Spray a bit more oil and add the green onions to it.
5. Stir fry the onions until they are half cooked, now add the tomato cubes to the onions and mix
6. Continue to cook for a few more seconds while you add the soy sauce, stevia, and salt to it.
7. Mix it well and cook until the tomatoes are soft and slightly mushy.
8. Now add the scrambled eggs to the pan and mix thoroughly.
9. Increase the heat to maximum and cook away the extra liquid.
10. Transfer to a plate and serve hot. Enjoy!

Baked Chicken with Cherry Tomatoes and Peppers

Servings: 4

Type: Dinner

Ingredients:

- 4 chicken thighs (boneless)
- 1 cup chicken broth or water
- 6 cherry tomatoes (cut them into half)
- 2 teaspoon Italian herbs
- 2 garlic cloves
- 2 bell peppers (chopped)
- 1 tablespoon olive oil
- Salt and pepper, to taste

Method:

1. Preheat the oven to 350 degrees Fahrenheit
2. Spread the chicken thighs in an oven dish evenly
3. Place the chopped peppers and halved tomatoes over the chicken thighs
4. Season it with salt, pepper and Italian herbs.
5. Drizzle the olive oil over the contents and add the chicken broth or water over it.
6. Mix once and bake the contents for an hour until the meat browns and the vegetables soften.
7. Remove from oven and transfer to a plate.
8. Serve warm and enjoy!

Baked Chicken with Vegetables

Servings: 4

Type: Dinner

Ingredients:

- 4 chicken drumsticks
- 3 cherry tomatoes (cut into half)
- 1 zucchini (chopped)
- 2 garlic cloves
- 1 onion (diced)
- 1 red pepper (diced)
- 1/2 tablespoon sweet paprika
- 1 tablespoon oregano
- 1/2 tablespoon garlic powder
- 1 tablespoon olive oil
- Salt and pepper, to taste

Method:

1. Preheat oven to 350 degrees Fahrenheit
2. Spread the halved tomatoes, chopped zucchini, diced onion, and pepper in a tray
3. Take a small bowl and combine together olive oil, garlic powder, oregano, paprika, salt, and pepper.
4. Brush this olive spice mix over the chicken drumsticks and place them over the vegetables in the tray.
5. Toss the meat and vegetable once.
6. Transfer this to an oven-safe pot and pour a cup of water in it. Add the garlic cloves
7. Cover the pot and let it cook in the oven for 45 minutes.
8. Remove the lid and cook for another 15 minutes.

9. Transfer the cooked meat and veggie mix to a plate and serve hot. Enjoy!

Zero Carb Pizza

Servings: 2

Type: Breakfast

Ingredients:

- 7 ounces eggplant
- 2 thinly sliced tomatoes (medium ones) – should be sliced in ring-shape
- 3 1/2 ounces mozzarella cheese (fat-free)
- 1 1/2ounce bacon (low fat)
- 1 tablespoon quark cheese
- Italian seasoning, to taste

Method:

1. Preheat oven to 374 degrees Fahrenheit
2. Cut the eggplant into half and slice it into big thin slices.
3. Similarly, chop the mozzarella into thin slices
4. Spread the quark cheese on the top part of the eggplant slices so that it is moist.
5. Sprinkle the Italian seasoning over the cheese and place 3 tomato rings on each eggplant slice.
6. Now, place the mozzarella slices over the tomatoes and top it with low-fat bacon.
7. You can add more seasoning if required
8. Bake for 15 minutes until the veggies soften and become tender.
9. The cheese will melt over the veggies.
10. Transfer to a plate and serve warm. Enjoy!

Curried Ground Beef

Servings: 4

Type: Lunch

Ingredients:

- 1 pound ground beef (95% lean)
- 1 minced garlic clove
- 2 teaspoon allspice curry powder
- 1 teaspoon olive oil
- Salt and pepper, to taste

Method:

1. Heat the oil in a large skillet over medium-high heat.
2. Add the garlic to the hot oil and cook until the raw flavor goes
3. Now add the ground beef to the garlic in the skillet and let it cook for 30 minutes until the pink stains are gone.
4. Break down the meat into smaller pieces using a spatula or back of the spoon as it cooks.
5. Sprinkle the curry powder, salt, and pepper over the meat. Mix well until the flavors are well incorporated.
6. Cook for another 15 to 20 minutes until the contents are thoroughly cooked.
7. Transfer to a plate and serve hot. Enjoy!

Baked Buffalo Chicken Wings

Servings: 8

Type: Lunch

Ingredients:

- 4 tablespoons Buffalo Hot sauce (any brand or homemade)
- 2 pounds chicken wings (frozen)
- Nonstick cooking spray

Method:

1. Take a microwave-safe container and place the chicken wings in it.
2. Add water to it until the wings are halfway covered with water.
3. Microwave this for 10 minutes on high.
4. Remove the container; stir the contents and microwave again on high for another 10 minutes.
5. Preheat the oven to 425 degrees Fahrenheit.
6. Remove the chicken wings from the microwave and drain them.
7. Place them on a paper towel and let it cool. Slowly pat them dry and set aside
8. Grease a baking tray with nonstick cooking spray and keep ready.
9. Place the chicken wings on the tray in a single layer. Cover the tray with aluminum foil
10. Bake this for 40 to 45 minutes, then uncover and flip the wings.
11. Bake for another 10 to 15 minutes until the chicken wings are completely cooked

12. Remove from tray and let it cool for around 10 minutes
13. Transfer the chicken wings to a large bowl and pour the sauce (as per your taste) over the wings.
14. Toss it well and serve warm. Enjoy!

Mustard Egg Salad

Servings: 4

Type: Breakfast

Ingredients:

- 8 chopped hard-boiled eggs (5 egg whites and 3 whole eggs)
- 3 tablespoons parsley (finely chopped)
- 3 finely chopped scallions
- 1/2 cup celery (chopped)
- 1/4 teaspoon cumin
- 4 tablespoons Greek yogurt (non-fat)
- 1/2 teaspoon red pepper flakes
- 2 teaspoons mustard (whole grain)
- Salt and pepper, to taste

Method:

1. Mix together the mustard, red pepper flakes and cumin in a large bowl.
2. Add the chopped hard-boiled eggs into the bowl and give it a toss.
3. Add the yogurt to the coated eggs and mix well until the spices blend well
4. Sprinkle salt and pepper over the contents. Stir well.
5. Add the parsley, scallions, and celery to the bowl.
6. Mix thoroughly until all the ingredients are well incorporated.
7. If you want a creamier hot salad, add more Greek yogurt and red pepper flakes,
8. Transfer to a plate and serve cold! Enjoy!

Collard Green Quiche

Servings: 4

Type: Lunch

Ingredients:

- 1 1/2 cups collard greens (cooked)
- 3 eggs (large ones)
- 1/2 cup skim milk
- 2 egg whites
- 1/2 cup onion (chopped)
- 2 tablespoons cheddar cheese (reduced-fat)
- Salt and pepper, to taste
- Nonstick cooking spray

Method:
1. Preheat the oven to 375 degrees Fahrenheit
2. Grease a frying pan with nonstick cooking spray and heat it
3. Add onions and collard greens to the hot pan
4. Allow the veggies to be cooked for around 10 minutes until they all soften up and become tender
5. Take a large bowl and crack the 3 eggs into it.
6. Add the skimmed milk, egg whites, cheddar cheese, salt and pepper to the cracked eggs
7. Mix together until the contents are well blended
8. Grease a round baking dish and keep ready.
9. Add the cooked vegetables to the egg mixture and mix well.
10. Pour this into the baking dish and let it bake for 30 minutes until the contents are cooked thoroughly. The egg will begin to set basically
11. Transfer to a plate and serve cold or warm. Enjoy!

Lemongrass Tofu Stir-fry

Servings: 2

Type: Dinner

Ingredients:

- 8 ounces firm Tofu
- 2 zucchini (sliced)
- 5 ounces broccoli (cut into small florets)
- 1 teaspoon lemongrass (crushed)
- 1 garlic cloves (finely chopped)
- 1 teaspoon low-sodium soy sauce
- 1 teaspoon ginger (freshly grated)
- Juice of 1 lemon
- Nonstick cooking spray

Method:

1. Mix together the lemongrass, garlic, soy sauce, ginger and lemon juice in a small bowl. Set it aside.
2. Chop the tofu evenly into bite-sized chunks and set aside.
3. Grease a nonstick frying pan with cooking spray and heat it.
4. Place the chopped tofu to the hot pan and cook on high heat. Keep stirring often to prevent the tofu from sticking or burning
5. Add the sliced zucchini and broccoli to the pan once the tofu is lightly browned
6. Steam-fry the vegetables by adding two tablespoons of water.
7. Keep stirring continuously and let it cook until the veggies are firm but cooked well.

8. Pour the mixed lemongrass sauce over the tofu and vegetables.
9. Mix them thoroughly and cook for 2 more minutes until the sauce heats through
10. Transfer to a plate and serve hot. Enjoy!

Mexican Eggs

Servings: 2

Type: Dinner or Breakfast

Ingredients:

- 2 eggs
- 7 ounces canned tomatoes (chopped)
- 1 brown onion (thinly sliced)
- 1/2 bell peppers (red or yellow), chopped
- 1/2-teaspoon sweet paprika.
- 1/4 teaspoon chili
- 1/2 teaspoon oregano
- 1 teaspoon coriander (freshly chopped)
- 1/2 teaspoon ground cumin
- Nonstick cooking spray
- Salt and pepper, to taste

Method:

1. Heat a greased non-stick frying pan (using cooking spray) over medium heat.
2. Add onions to the hot pan and sauté for 10 minutes until it starts to brown.
3. Now, add the chopped bell pepper to the sautéed onions and let it cook for 2 to 3 minutes
4. Add paprika, chili, oregano, and cumin over the bell pepper and onions in the pan.
5. Mix well and let it cook until the spices turn fragrant
6. Now, add the canned tomatoes, pepper and salt to the contents in the pan.
7. Mix slowly and cook on low heat for around 5 minutes.

8. You can add a splash of water if the sauce is thickening and get stuck to the bottom of the pan.
9. Now, make two big-enough hollows in the sauce and crack the eggs into the two pits.
10. When you crack your eggs, they will be sitting on the bottom of the pan surrounded by the sauce (not on the sauce but on the pan)
11. Increase the heat to medium-high and let the eggs cook for 6 minutes until the whites firm up and the yolk starts to run.
12. Garnish with the chopped coriander and transfer to a plate.
13. Serve warm and enjoy!

Microwave Spaghetti Squash

Servings: 4

Type: Lunch

Ingredients:

- 1 spaghetti squash (medium)
- 1 pound ground chicken
- 2 cups spinach
- 1/2 minced onion
- 2 tablespoons soy sauce
- 3 minced garlic cloves,
- 2 tablespoons sriracha
- 1 teaspoon olive oil
- Nonstick cooking spray

Method:
1. Pierce all over the squash with a fork and place it in the microwave.
2. Microwave for 10 minutes until the vegetable becomes soft
3. Heat the olive oil over medium heat in a sauté pan and add the garlic to the hot oil
4. Allow it to cook until the raw flavor goes; now add the onions to the pan and sauté.
5. Cook for around 5 minutes until the onion becomes translucent and soft.
6. Add the spinach to the pan and carefully mix the contents.
7. Cook for 2 more minutes and add the ground chicken to the contents in the pan.
8. Continue to stir as the meat and vegetable get cooked.

9. You can break the ground chicken into smaller pieces if they are too big or large.
10. Continue to cook until the chicken browns and is completely cooked.
11. Now add the soy sauce and sriracha to the cooked meat and veggies. Stir them together until well combined.
12. Reduce the heat and simmer for 2 minutes.
13. Meanwhile cut the spaghetti squash in half and scoop out the spaghetti from both the halves.
14. Add this to the pan and stir once.
15. Transfer to a plate and serve hot or warm. Enjoy!

Middle Eastern Meatballs

Servings: 4

Type: Lunch

Ingredients:

- 1 pound lean ground beef (5-10% fat)
- 1 egg
- 1/4 onion (chopped)
- 2 garlic cloves (minced)
- 1 tablespoon mint (freshly chopped)
- 1/2 tablespoon smoked paprika
- 3 tablespoons flat leaf parsley (chopped)
- 1 tablespoon coriander
- 2 tablespoons dill (freshly chopped)
- 1 tablespoon cumin
- Salt and pepper (freshly ground), to taste
- Nonstick cooking spray

Method:

1. Preheat oven to 450 degrees Fahrenheit.
2. Grease the baking tray with nonstick cooking spray and set aside
3. Take a large bowl and crack the egg into it.
4. Add the beef, onion, garlic to the cracked egg and mix thoroughly
5. Now, add the mint, paprika, parsley, coriander, dill, cumin, salt and pepper to the contents in the bowl.
6. Using your hands, mix them gently as over-mixing will make the mixture toughen
7. Make 16 meatballs from the mixture and place them neatly on the greased baking tray

8. Bake for 20 to 30 minutes until the meatballs are thoroughly cooked and turn brown
9. Transfer to a plate and serve hot. Enjoy!

Chapter Eight: Stabilization Phase Recipes

Slow Cooker Rotisserie Chicken

Servings: 4-6

Type: Lunch

Ingredients:

- 3 pounds chicken (1 whole), cleaned and fat removed
- 1 lemon (cut into half)
- 1 teaspoon smoked paprika
- 1/2 teaspoon garlic powder
- 1/2 teaspoon dried oregano
- 1/2 teaspoon salt
- 1/2 teaspoon dried basil
- 1/2 teaspoon pepper

Method:

1. Make around 5 balls from aluminum foil and place them in the bottom of the slow cooker. Set aside.
2. Take a small bowl and mix together the spices – paprika, garlic powder, oregano, salt, basil and pepper with the juice of 1 lemon.
3. Rub the mixed spice all over the chicken. Now, place the two halves of the lemon (juice taken) into the cavity of the chicken
4. Place the spice-coated chicken over the aluminum foil balls in the slow cooker
5. Set the temperature on low and cook for 8 hours
6. Preheat the oven to 500 degrees Fahrenheit.
7. Place the cooked chicken in a baking tray and roast it in the oven for 10 minutes.
8. Transfer to a plate and serve the crispy chicken. Enjoy!

Fish Ceviche

Servings: 8

Type: Breakfast or dinner

Ingredients:

- 2 pounds red snapper fillets (firm and fresh), sliced into 1/2 inch squares
- 1/2 thinly sliced or grated red onion
- 1/2 cup lime juice
- 2 teaspoons salt
- 1/2 cup lemon juice
- Dash of hot sauce
- Dash of ground oregano
- Nonstick cooking spray

Method:

1. Take a medium-sized bowl and place the grated onion in it.
2. Add the lime juice, salt, lemon juice, oregano, and hot sauce to the onion.
3. Mix them well.
4. Add the chopped fillets to the contents in the bowl and gently mix them well.
5. The fish should be completely coated with the spiced juice.
6. Cover the bowl and refrigerate for an hour
7. Preheat the oven to 325 degrees Fahrenheit
8. Grease a baking tray with nonstick cooking spray and set aside.
9. Spread the coated fish evenly in the greased baking tray and place it in the oven.

10. Cook for an hour until the fish is completely cooked and slightly crispy.
11. Transfer to a plate and serve hot

Cauliflower Soup

Servings: 8

Type: Breakfast or dinner

Ingredients:

- 1 fresh cauliflower (large head)
- 1 finely sliced medium onion
- 4 1/2 cups hot water, divided
- 1 teaspoon fresh thyme
- Salt and black pepper, to taste
- 1 teaspoon olive oil

Method:
1. Heat the olive oil in a large pot over medium-low heat.
2. Add the onion to the hot pot and cook for 15 minutes until they become translucent and soft
3. Pour one cup of water to the pot and add the cauliflower to it (you can trim the cauliflower and cut them into large chunks).
4. Season it with salt and pepper. Increase the heat to medium and cover the pot.
5. Simmer it down and allow the contents to cook for around 15 minutes until the cauliflower is tender and soft.
6. Pour the remaining water and add the thyme to the pot.
7. Continue to simmer for another 20 minutes.
8. Use an immersion blender and puree the soup as it simmers.
9. Turn off the heat and let it sit for 20 minutes for the soup to thicken up.
10. Transfer to a bowl and serve warm. Enjoy!

Mushroom Omelet

Servings: 1

Type: Breakfast

Ingredients:

- 2 ounce cleaned and sliced mushrooms
- 1 egg
- 2 egg whites
- 1 minced garlic clove
- 2 tablespoons cheese (fat-free)
- 1 tablespoon milk (non-fat)
- 1/2 teaspoon minced fresh thyme
- 1 teaspoon chives (chopped)
- 2 teaspoon parsley (chopped)
- Salt and pepper, to taste
- Nonstick cooking spray

Method:

1. Grease a nonstick skillet with cooking spray and heat it over medium-high heat.
2. Add mushrooms to the hot skillet and stir-fry it for 3 minutes
3. Now, add the garlic, thyme, pepper, and salt to the mushrooms in the skillet,
4. Stir together and cook for another minute. Once done, set it aside.
5. Take a medium-sized bowl and crack the egg into it.
6. Add the egg whites, milk, chives, parsley and pepper to the cracked eggs.
7. Whisk them all together until blended well.
8. Heat another greased nonstick pan over medium heat.

9. Pour the egg mixture into the hot pan and let it cook for 3 to 5 minutes until the edges are crispy.
10. Flip over to the other side and cook for another 2 minutes
11. Place the cooked mushroom on the plate and sprinkle the cheese over it.
12. Fold the omelet into half and slide to a plate
13. Serve warm and enjoy!

Deviled Eggs

Servings: 24 egg halves

Type: Breakfast

Ingredients:

- 12 large eggs
- 2 tablespoons green onions (chopped)
- 1/2 cup plain Greek yogurt (fat-free)
- 2 teaspoons hot pepper sauce
- 1/8 teaspoon paprika
- 1 tablespoon Dijon mustard
- 1/8 teaspoon salt
- 1/8 teaspoon black pepper

Method:

1. Place the eggs in a large saucepan and cover them with water.
2. Bring the water to boil and wait until the eggs are boiled (around 5 to 10 minutes)
3. Remove from heat and cover the saucepan. Let it sit for 15 minutes.
4. Transfer the eggs to a plate and allow it to cool
5. Peel the eggs once they have cooled and slice them in half.
6. Separate the yolks and egg whites. Save 6 yolks and use the remaining for some other recipe.
7. Take a medium-sized bowl and combine together the yogurt, pepper sauce, paprika, Dijon, salt, pepper and the egg yolks in it. Mix them well enough.
8. Take one tablespoon of the yolk-spice mix and fill it in the yolk-space of the egg white.
9. Garnish with green onions and serve immediately. Enjoy!

Roasted Crepe Quesadillas

Servings: 1

Type: Breakfast

Ingredients:

- 2 slices Canadian bacon
- 1 egg white
- 1/4 cup cheese (fat-free or low fat)
- 1 whole egg
- Salt and pepper, to taste
- Nonstick cooking spray

Method:

1. Take a medium-sized bowl and crack the egg.
2. Add the egg white, salt, and pepper to the cracked egg.
3. Whisk them together and set it aside
4. Grease a nonstick frying pan with cooking spray and heat it over medium heat.
5. Pour the egg mixture into the pan and twist the pan slowly so as to evenly distribute the egg mixture all through the pan
6. Allow it to cook for 2 minutes until you see bubbles coming.
7. When the top of egg almost cooks through, flip over to the other side using a spatula
8. Sprinkle the cheese over the egg and place the bacon slice on top it. Sprinkle bit more cheese over the slice.
9. Fold the crepe in half after 30 seconds such that it covers the bacon and cheese
10. Cook the crepe until the cheese melts and transfer it to a plate

11. Slice the crepe into triangles (since you already folded the crepe, just cut in the middle) and serve immediately.
12. Enjoy!

Ginger Salmon

Servings: 2

Type: Dinner

Ingredients:

- 2 salmon fillets (6 ounces each fillet)
- 1 tbsp minced fresh ginger
- 1/4 cup rice vinegar
- 2 cloves crushed garlic
- 1/2 packet Stevia
- 1/2 tsp hot chili sauce
- 1/4 cup water
- 1 tsp soy sauce
- Nonstick cooking spray

Method:

1. Take a small bowl and pour the rice vinegar in it
2. Add the fresh ginger, crushed garlic, stevia, chili sauce, soy sauce and water to the bowl.
3. Whisk them all together until the contents are well-blended
4. Marinate the fillets with this sauce mixture in the same bowl and cover it with an aluminum foil. Let it sit for 30 minutes.
5. Heat a greased saucepan (use cooking spray) over medium-high heat.
6. Place the marinated fillets in the hot pan and roast it for 4 minutes until the salmon is flaky.
7. Flip the fillets over and cook for another 4 minutes until the fish is completely cooked.
8. Transfer to a plate and serve warm. Enjoy!

Cauliflower Rice

Servings: 2

Type: Lunch or Dinner

Ingredients:

- 1 whole head of the cauliflower
- 2 tablespoons chopped onions
- 2 tablespoons chopped shallots
- 2 minced garlic cloves
- 1 teaspoon olive oil
- 1 teaspoon mixed herbs
- 1/2 tablespoon basil (freshly crushed)
- Salt and Pepper, to taste

Method:

1. Trim the cauliflower and cut the heat into chunks
2. Transfer the cauliflower chunks to a food processor and pulse it for 30 to 45 seconds until you get the texture of rice.
3. Don't over pulse as it will become a paste if done so
4. Heat oil in a large skillet over medium heat.
5. Add the garlic and onions to the hot oil, sauté for a minute until the raw flavor of the garlic goes and the onions become translucent
6. Add the shallots to the contents in the skillet and continue to sauté.
7. Now, add the pulsed cauliflower and cook for 5 to 10 minutes until it becomes soft like cooked rice
8. Season with mixed herbs, basil, salt, and pepper. Mix well until the flavors are well blended.
9. Transfer to a plate and serve hot or warm along with gravy of your choice.
10. Enjoy!

Miso Soup

Servings: 2

Type: Breakfast

Ingredients:

- 1 tablespoon white miso paste
- 2 cups vegetable or chicken broth
- 2 chopped scallions
- 2 tablespoons dried seaweed
- 1 teaspoon dashi granules

Method:

1. Pour the vegetable or chicken broth into a soup pot and bring it to boil
2. Add the dashi granules and the miso paste to the boiling soup
3. Reduce the heat and let it simmer for 5 to 10 minutes
4. Carefully whisk the mixture using an immersion blender to get a thick consistency
5. Add the scallions and dried seaweed to the whisked soup
6. Simmer for 2 to 3 minutes and turn off the heat
7. Transfer to a bowl and serve hot. Enjoy!

Oat Bran Crackers

Servings: 4

Type: Breakfast or Snack

Ingredients:

- 1 cup oat bran
- 2 teaspoons active yeast
- 1 teaspoon olive oil
- 1 cup warm water
- 1/4 teaspoon salt
- Pepper, to taste

Method:

1. Take a medium-sized bowl and pour the warm water into it.
2. Add the yeast to the warm water and let it rest for around 10 minutes until it starts bubbling
3. Now, add the oat bran, olive oil, pinch of pepper and salt to the yeast water.
4. Mix together thoroughly until you get a sticky dough consistency
5. Make a ball out of the dough and cover it with a paper towel or kitchen towel.
6. Let it sit for an hour so that the dough rises
7. Grease a baking sheet with parchment paper and set aside.
8. Preheat the oven to 430 degrees Fahrenheit and place the greased baking sheet in it
9. Place two sheets of parchment paper on the kitchen counter and place the dough on it.

10. Roll the dough to form a 16 x 16 square carefully. The parchment paper will prevent the dough from sticking.
11. Now, cut the flattened dough into 32 equal squares
12. Remove the hot baking tray from the oven and place a new parchment on it.
13. Place the 32 crackers (squares) on the tray and bake it for 10 minutes
14. Remove from the oven and flip the crackers to the other side.
15. Bake for another 10 minutes until the crackers are crispy and dry
16. Let it cool for some time and then transfer to the plate.
17. Serve and enjoy!

Mint & Curry Omelet

Servings: 2

Type: Breakfast or Dinner

Ingredients:

- 2 tablespoons chopped fresh mint
- 1/4 cup quark
- 2 teaspoons curry powder
- 4 eggs
- Salt and Pepper, to taste
- Nonstick cooking spray

Method:

1. Take a medium-sized bowl and crack the eggs into it.
2. Add the quark to the cracked eggs and whisk them together until blended
3. Add the curry powder, salt, and pepper to the whisked mixture.
4. Stir well and carefully fold the chopped mint to the mixture
5. Grease a nonstick frying pan with cooking spray and heat it.
6. Spoon the egg curry mixture to the hot pan and spread it to a round shape.
7. Cook for 3 to 5 minutes until the edges are crispy and the egg sets
8. Flip the omelet using a spatula and cook for another 3 minutes
9. Slide the omelet to a plate and serve hot!
10. Repeat steps 6 to 9 with the remaining egg mixture.

Meat Salad

Servings: 2

Type: Breakfast or Dinner

Ingredients:

- 1 chicken breast (cooked) - leftovers
- 1 Egg yolk
- 1/2 pound turkey mince
- 1 tablespoon yogurt (fat-free)
- 2 slices turkey ham
- 1/2 tablespoon Dijon mustard
- 1 tablespoon chili seasoning
- 1 tablespoon skim ricotta cheese (low-fat)
- Nonstick cooking spray

Method:

1. Take a medium-sized bowl and place the egg yolk in it.
2. Add the yogurt and skim ricotta to the yolk in the bowl.
3. Blend them all together until smooth and creamy
4. Grease a frying pan with cooking spray and heat it.
5. Add the ground turkey to the hot pan and pan fry it.
6. Add the chili seasoning and continue to cook until it is browned.
7. Add the turkey ham along with the Dijon mustard and pan fry it for 5 minutes until slightly browned.
8. Add the leftover cooked chicken breast to the turkey mixture and stir it once.
9. Let it cook for 1 or 2 minutes until the chicken is heated through.
10. Break the ham into small chunks using the back of the spoon.

11. Pour the creamy mixture to the meat and combine once until the contents are incorporated.
12. Turn off the heat and let it sit for a while.
13. Serve warm or cold. Enjoy!

Creamy Mushroom Soup

Servings: 3

Type: Breakfast

Ingredients:

- 17 ounces fresh mushrooms (washed and sliced)
- 2 cups chicken broth
- 1 onion (coarsely chopped)
- 1 carrot (tolerated), sliced
- 1 bouquet of herbs (tarragon, sage, and/or basil)
- 1/2 celery (coarsely chopped)
- 1 cup fresh cream (3% fat)
- Salt and pepper, to taste
- Olive oil, to grease

Method:

1. Clean the herbs, pat dry and set them aside
2. Heat a large heavy-bottomed saucepan over medium-high heat
3. Add few drops of olive oil and spread it all over the bottom of the pan
4. Pour the chicken broth into the pan and add the vegetables (onion, carrot, celery, and mushrooms) to it.
5. Make a bouquet of the herbs and add the herb bouquet to the pan
6. Bring it to a boil and reduce the heat to low. Cover the pan and simmer for 10 to 15 minutes until the veggies and mushrooms are cooked well.
7. Turn off heat and discard the herb bouquet.
8. Puree the soup in a blender until creamy and smooth

9. If you like to have chunks of vegetables in the soup, take out the onions and few mushrooms before you blend. Then add them back to the creamy soup
10. Add the fresh cream and mix well. Season with salt and pepper.
11. Transfer to a bowl and serve warm. Enjoy!

Chicken and Zucchini Moussaka

Servings: 2

Type: Lunch

Ingredients:

- 8 ounces chicken breast (minced)
- 2 chopped green onions
- 14 ounces zucchini slices
- 1 egg
- 6 cherry tomatoes (chopped)
- 1/2 cup lean broth
- 3 tablespoons parsley (chopped)
- 3 tablespoons skim milk
- Salt and pepper, to taste
- 1 tablespoon olive oil

Method:

1. Heat oil in a saucepan over medium heat and add the onions to it.
2. Sauté the onions for 5 minutes until they are soft and translucent
3. Add the minced chicken, pepper, and salt to the onions in the pan.
4. Cook for 5 minutes as you continue to stir.
5. Add the tomatoes and parsley to the contents in the pan. Stir well and continue to cook for another 5 minutes until the tomatoes become soft and mushy
6. Pour the broth over the vegetables and increase the heat to medium-high.
7. Cook for 10 more minutes until the contents are thoroughly cooked

8. Line a casserole dish with parchment paper and preheat the oven to 356 degrees Fahrenheit.
9. Place the zucchini slices in a neat uniform layer and spread the cooked mixture over the top.
10. Continue with another layer of zucchini slices and season with salt and pepper.
11. Take a small bowl and crack the eggs.
12. Add the skim milk to the cracked eggs and beat the mixture until smooth and thick.
13. Pour the egg-milk mixture over the zucchini.
14. Place the casserole dish in the oven and bake for 30 minutes until the eggs are set and the contents are heated through
15. Transfer to a plate and serve warm. Enjoy!

Chapter Nine: Dukan Vegetarian Recipes

Baked Mashed Cauliflower

Servings: 4

Ingredients:

- 1 cauliflower (medium or large)
- 1 teaspoon paprika
- 2 tablespoons yogurt (Zero-fat)
- Salt & pepper, to taste

Method:
1. Trim the cauliflower and break them into florets.
2. Steam the florets in salted water until soft and tender
3. Transfer the steamed cauliflower to a high-speed blender and add pepper to it.
4. Blend for 30 seconds until smooth.
5. Add the yogurt and salt to the cauliflower puree. Blend again for another 30 seconds.

6. Transfer this to an ovenproof dish and set aside.
7. Preheat the oven to its highest temperature.
8. Sprinkle the paprika over the cauliflower and bake this for 5 minutes until the top part has slightly browned.
9. Turn off and remove from the oven. Transfer to a plate and serve warm. Enjoy!

Parsnip and Cauliflower Mash Up

Servings: 4

Ingredients:

- 15 ounces parsnips (peeled and chopped)
- 4 tablespoons Crème Fraiche (zero fat)
- 1 small cauliflower (broken into florets)
- Salt and pepper, to taste
- 2 minced garlic cloves

Method:

1. Steam the chopped parsnips and cauliflower florets together until they are soft and tender
2. Transfer the steamed veggies to a high-process blender.
3. Add the minced garlic, salt, and pepper to the veggies, and blend for 30 seconds until smooth
4. Add the crème Fraiche to the mashed cauliflower and parsnips to the blender.
5. Blend for another 30 seconds and transfer to a bowl.
6. Serve warm and enjoy!

Garlicky Cauliflower Mash

Servings: 4

Ingredients:

- 1 medium cauliflower
- 1 teaspoon minced garlic
- 1 teaspoon fresh chives (chopped)
- Salt and black pepper (freshly ground), to taste
- 3 tablespoons Greek yogurt (zero-fat)

Method:

1. Trim the cauliflower and break the florets.
2. Steam the cauliflower florets until soft but crisp
3. Transfer the steamed cauliflower to the blender and add the minced garlic, salt, pepper and yogurt to it.
4. Blend on high for 30 to 45 seconds until creamy and smooth.
5. Transfer to a bowl and garnish with chopped chives
6. Serve warm and enjoy!

Dukan Cauliflower Pizza

Servings: 2

Ingredients:

- 2 cups cauliflower rice (cold cooked)
- 2 Light Babybel cheese
- 1 egg
- 1 tablespoon oat bran
- 1 egg white
- Salt and pepper, to taste
- Olive oil, for greasing

For toppings
- 2 tablespoons tomato puree
- 2 tablespoon low-fat grated cheese (any kind)
- 1 cup chopped vegetables (bell peppers, tomato, zucchini or any other veggies you desire)
- 1 teaspoon dried mixed herbs
- 1/2 teaspoon dried oregano
- 1/2 teaspoon fresh basil (finely chopped)

Method:

1. Grate the Babybel cheese into a bowl.
2. Add the oat bran and the cooked cauliflower rice to the cheese in the bowl.
3. Mix well until the contents are well-combined
4. Crack the egg into it and add the egg white.
5. Mix well to form a dough consistency
6. Add the salt and pepper to the dough, and mix to ensure the flavors are blended well
7. Preheat the oven to 400 degrees Fahrenheit
8. Grease a baking sheet with few drops of olive oil.

9. Transfer the pizza to the greased baking sheet and spread it around thin or thick (based on how you want)
10. You can roll over the edges if you want
11. Bake the pizza for 15 minutes (if thin) or 30 minutes (if thick) until the edges of the crust looks crunchy
12. Remove from the oven and let it sit for a minute or two
13. Top it with tomato puree, chopped vegetables, and grated cheese. Sprinkle over with mixed herbs, oregano, and fresh basil
14. Return the pizza back to the oven and bake for another 15 minutes until the cheese melts and the vegetables are cooked.
15. Remove from the oven and slice the pizza.
16. Transfer to a plate and serve hot. Enjoy!

Sautéed Green Beans

Servings: 6

Ingredients:

- 1 1/2 pounds trimmed green beans
- 1 garlic clove (finely chopped)
- 1 tablespoon shallots (finely chopped)
- 1 teaspoon lemon zest
- Freshly ground black pepper and salt, to taste

Method:

1. Heat a shallow frying pan on medium-high heat.
2. Pour water into it and add the green beans.
3. Reduce the heat and let it simmer for 5 minutes
4. Remove the beans from the heat, drain them and blanch them by placing them under cold running water or putting them in a bowl of ice cold water
5. Add the shallots and garlic in the same frying pan and dry fry it with a splash of water (if required)
6. Let it cook for 3 to 5 minutes until the garlic and shallots become soft.
7. Add the beans now and continue to cook for another 3 minutes.
8. Sprinkle with salt and pepper and give the contents a stir.
9. Remove from heat and add the lemon zest.
10. Mix them well until the flavors are well incorporated. Transfer to a plate and serve warm. Enjoy!

Carrot and Butternut Squash Puree

Servings: 6

Ingredients:

- 1 pound carrots (peeled and sliced)
- 1/8 teaspoon nutmeg
- 1 pound butternut squash (peeled and cubed)
- Freshly ground black pepper and salt, to taste

Method:

1. Steam the squash and carrots until soft and tender
2. Once done, transfer the steamed veggies to a food processor or high-speed blender.
3. Add the nutmeg to it and blend until smooth and creamy – it will need to be in a puree consistency
4. Transfer to a bowl and season with salt and black pepper.
5. Serve warm and enjoy!

Baked Zucchini Chips

Servings: 4

Ingredients:

- 1 large zucchini
- 1 teaspoon olive oil
- Sea salt and pepper, to taste
- 1/2 teaspoon red chili flakes

Method:

1. Preheat oven to 225 degrees Fahrenheit
2. Chop the zucchini into thin slices in round shape (like a medallion) or lengthwise into strips (if the zucchini is not too big)
3. Take a small piece of aluminum foil and brush olive oil on it (thin coat).
4. Place the zucchini over the oily foil to oil the slices (repeat for all the sliced pieces and brush with more oil if required)
5. Spread the oil-coated zucchini on a parchment-lined baking tray such that the oil side of the slices faces up.
6. Mix together the red chili flakes, sea salt and pepper in a small bowl until well combined.
7. Sprinkle this spice mix over the zucchini sparingly and place the tray in the oven
8. Bake for 45 minutes until the zucchini becomes crisp and crunchy
9. Check in between and flip the sides to ensure even cooking is done.
10. Remove from the oven and let it cool. Transfer to a plate and serve warm. Enjoy!

Chapter Ten: Dukan Soup Recipes

Carrot and Zucchini Soup

Servings: 4

Ingredients:

- 1 pound carrots (peeled and sliced)
- 1 medium onion (finely chopped)
- 1 pound zucchini (unpeeled and sliced)
- 3 1/2 cups vegetable or chicken stock
- 2 teaspoons curry powder
- Sprigs of parsley, to garnish.
- A handful of parsley, freshly chopped
- Salt and pepper, to taste

Method:

1. Heat a nonstick frying pan over medium heat.
2. Add the onions and dry fry them until translucent and soft.
3. You can add a bit of stock while frying the onions if you desire

4. Add the zucchini and carrots to the pan mix them well and continue to cook.
5. Add the curry powder and pour the stock over the vegetables.
6. Bring the contents to boil and reduce the heat to low.
7. Simmer the veggies for 20 minutes until they are tender and cooked
8. Add the chopped parsley and sprinkle some salt and pepper. Mix well until the flavors combine
9. Use a hand blender to blend the soup while it is simmering.
10. When it becomes thick and creamy, stir the contents one last time and turn off the heat.
11. Garnish the parsley sprig over the soup and transfer the contents to a bowl.
12. Serve hot or warm and enjoy!

Tofu Noodle Soup

Servings: 2

Ingredients:

- 6 ounces firm tofu (cubed)
- 6 finely sliced mushrooms
- 3 fluid ounces vegetable stock
- 2 shredded spring onions
- 1 teaspoon fresh ginger (chopped)
- 1 3/4 ounces shirataki noodles
- 1 finely chopped garlic clove
- 1 teaspoon mint or basil leaves (finely chopped)
- 1/4 chili flakes, to serve
- 2 teaspoon soy sauce + extra, for serving
- Salt and pepper, to taste

Method:

1. Heat a shallow pan over medium heat and pour the vegetable stock into it.
2. Add the tofu cubes and simmer for around 5 minutes.
3. Now, add the ginger and garlic to the pan and bring the contents to boil.
4. Reduce the heat to low and simmer for another 20 minutes (partly cover the pan)
5. Now, add the noodles and cook for around 5 minutes.
6. Add the mushrooms, soy sauce and half the spring onions to the pan.
7. Allow it to simmer for 4 to 5 minutes until the noodles are soft and cooked.
8. Sprinkle salt and pepper, mix the contents well and cook for 2 more minutes.
9. Remove from heat and transfer the soup to a bowl.

10. Sprinkle few spring onions from the reserved, basil leaves, chili flakes and a bit of soy sauce.
11. Serve warm and enjoy!

Roasted Red Pepper and Carrot Soup

Servings: 4

Ingredients:

- 2 red bell peppers (large ones)
- 3 large carrots (peeled and sliced)
- 4 garlic cloves (peeled and diced)
- 1 large onion (sliced)
- 1 bay leaf
- 1/2 teaspoon curry powder
- 1 teaspoon olive oil
- Sea salt and black pepper (freshly ground), to taste

Method:

1. Preheat the oven to 350 degrees Fahrenheit
2. Spread the bell pepper evenly on a baking sheet and let it roast for an hour until it blackens and the skin gets wrinkled.
3. Turn the peppers once in a while to check even cooking
4. Remove from the oven and transfer them to a bowl. Let it cool.
5. Peel off the skin from the cooled pepper and remove the seeds if there are any oil
6. Heat the oil over medium heat in a frying pan.
7. Add the bay leaf to the hot oil and then the curry powder.
8. Stir the contents for around 5 to 10 seconds and then add the onions and garlic to it.
9. Let it cook for 2 to 3 minutes until the raw flavor goes off from the garlic and the onion becomes soft and tender.

10. Now add the carrots, sprinkle some salt and stir well. Cook for 5 more minutes until the carrots change color and turn soft
11. Pour 4 cups of water to the veggies in the pan and then add the cooked peppers (deseeded and skinned).
12. Bring the contents to boil and then reduce the heat to low.
13. Simmer and continue to cook for 30 more minutes.
14. Discard the bay leaf and blend the mixture using an immersion blender carefully until smooth.
15. Transfer the creamy soup to a bowl and season it with pepper.
16. Serve hot and enjoy!

Moroccan Soup

Servings: 4

Ingredients:

- 3 1/2 ounces string beans (frozen)
- 1 chopped medium onion
- 14 ounces plum tomato with garlic, chopped (1 can)
- 2 1/2 cups hot vegetable stock
- 2 chopped celery sticks
- Zest and juice of half lemon
- 1 teaspoon olive oil
- 2 teaspoons cumin (ground)
- Large handful coriander or parsley (chopped), to serve
- Dukan bread slices (as you desire)
- Salt and black pepper, to taste

Method:

1. Heat the oil over medium heat in a large saucepan.
2. Add the chopped onions and celery to the hot oil.
3. Stir-fry for around 10 minutes until the onions turn translucent and celery becomes soft
4. Add the cumin and fry for one more minute. Increase the heat to medium-high.
5. Pour the vegetable stock over the onions and celery in the pan. Add the canned tomatoes and dash of pepper. Season with salt and bring the contents to boil.
6. Reduce the heat and simmer for around 8 minutes. Add the string beans and cook for 2 more minutes.
7. Now, add the lemon juice and stir once for the last time.

8. Remove from heat and sprinkle the lemon zest and parsley.
9. Transfer to a bowl and serve hot with the Dukan bread.
10. Enjoy!

Lumpy Dukan Miracle Soup

Servings: 4 to 6

Ingredients:

- 3 vegetable bouillon/stock cubes or chicken bouillon/stock cubes
- 2 cans chopped tomatoes
- Half cabbage head (coarsely chopped)
- 5 scallions (finely chopped), for garnishing
- 2 onions (large ones)
- 3 carrots (diced into large bite-size chunks)
- 2 green bell peppers (diced into large bite-size pieces)
- 1/2 teaspoon freshly ground black pepper or curry powder
- A head of celery, (coarsely chopped)
- Salt, to taste

Method:

1. Heat a large soup pot over medium-high heat.
2. Place all the vegetables (tomatoes, cabbage, onions, carrots, bell peppers, and celery) into the hot pot.
3. Pour water until the vegetables are completely immersed. Add salt to taste.
4. Bring the contents to boil and let it cook for 10 minutes.
5. Add the chicken stock cubes or vegetable stock cubes to the pot and cover.
6. Simmer for 15 minutes until the vegetables are soft and completely cooked
7. If you want the soup to be creamy and thick, blend the contents using an immersion blender as it simmers.

8. Sprinkle black pepper over the soup and stir well. Cook for 2 more minutes and turn off heat.
9. Transfer to the serving bowl and garnish with spring onions.
10. Serve warm and enjoy!

Spicy Roasted Turnip Soup

Servings: 4

Ingredients:

- 23 ounces diced turnip
- 1 large onion (chopped into 8 chunks)
- 2 quartered plum tomatoes
- 2 garlic cloves (peeled)
- 1 teaspoon ground coriander
- 5 cups vegetable stock
- 1/2 teaspoon mustard seeds
- 1/2 teaspoon ground turmeric
- 2 teaspoons olive oil
- 1 teaspoon cumin seeds
- 1 tablespoon lemon juice
- Salt and pepper, to taste

Method:

1. Preheat the oven to 428 degrees Fahrenheit
2. Take a large bowl and combine together the coriander, mustard, turmeric, cumin, and oil.
3. Add the turnip, onion, tomatoes, and garlic to the mixed spices.
4. Stir well until the spices and veggies are thoroughly mixed.
5. Spread the spice-coated vegetables on a heavy-bottomed baking tray and place in the oven
6. Roast for 30 minutes until the veggies are soft and tender
7. Transfer the vegetables into a food processor and add half of the vegetable stock into it.
8. Pulse the contents until smooth and thick.

9. Heat the remaining stock in a shallow pan over medium-high heat.
10. Add the pulsed vegetable soup into the stock in the pan and reduce the heat.
11. Season with salt and pepper, and let it simmer for 10 minutes
12. Turn off the heat and transfer to a serving bowl
13. Sprinkle more pepper if you want the soup to be hot and serve warm. Enjoy!

Creamy Smoked Salmon and Broccoli Soup

Servings: 4

Ingredients:

- 7 ounces smoked salmon (cut into strips)
- 4 cups vegetable or chicken stock
- 35 ounces broccoli (diced)
- 2 halved and finely sliced leeks (large ones)
- 3 1/3 fluid ounces buttermilk (low-fat)
- Small bunch chives (finely chopped)
- 1 bay leaf
- 1 teaspoon olive oil
- Salt and pepper, to taste

Method:

1. Heat the oil over medium heat in a large saucepan.
2. Add the bay leaf and leaks to the hot oil. Reduce the heat to low
3. Cook for 10 minutes until the leek is soft and tender.
4. Add the broccoli and stir the contents. Pour the stock over to the greens in the pan and mix again.
5. Add the buttermilk and simmer the contents for 19 minutes until the broccoli is soft and cooked. You will see the liquid bubbling as they simmer.
6. Add around two-thirds of the smoked almond into the pan and stir until the contents are combined well.
7. Season with salt and pepper, and let it cook for another 2 to 3 minutes.
8. Turn off the heat and discard the bay leaf.
9. Ladle the soup into the serving bowls and garnish with chives and the remaining smoked salmon.
10. Serve warm and enjoy!

Leftover Chicken Soup

Servings: 4

Ingredients:

- 10 ounces leftover roast chicken (skinless and shredded)
- 7 ounces mushrooms
- 6 cups chicken stock
- 3 chopped carrots (medium ones)
- 1 crushed garlic clove
- 2 chopped onions
- 3 tablespoons Greek yogurt (low fat)
- 1 tablespoon roughly chopped thyme leaves,
- 2 teaspoon olive oil
- 1 squeeze of lemon

Method:

1. Heat oil in a heavy-bottomed skillet over medium-high heat
2. Add the onions to the hot oil and sauté for 3 minutes until soft.
3. Add the thyme and carrot to the sautéed onions and stir-fry them for 12 minutes
4. Pour the stock and continue stirring the mixture.
5. Bring it to boil and cover the skillet. Reduce heat and let it simmer for 10 minutes
6. Add the chicken and continue to stir well.
7. Remove half of the contents from the skillet and set aside.
8. Use a stick blender to puree the removed content until smooth and thick.
9. Add this back to the skillet and mix well.

10. Now, add the mushrooms and let it cook for 5 minutes as you stir often
11. Mix the crushed garlic, yogurt and a squeeze of lemon in a separate small bowl and keep aside
12. Turn off the heat and transfer the cooked soup into a bowl. Now, add the yogurt mixture to the hot soup and mix once.
13. Serve warm and enjoy!

Thai Shirataki Noodle with Coconut and Salmon

Servings: 3

Ingredients:

- 3 1/2 ounces shirataki noodles
- 2 tablespoons Thai red curry paste
- 4 – 6 drops of coconut flavoring
- 2 skinless salmon (4.4 ounces each)
- 2 shredded spring onions
- 5 1/2 fluid ounces buttermilk (low-fat)
- 2 cups chicken stock
- 1 shredded red chili,
- 1 teaspoon fish sauce
- 1 tablespoon chopped fresh coriander
- Juice of 1 lime
- Nonstick cooking spray
- Salt and pepper, to taste

Method:

1. Grease a nonstick saucepan and heat it over medium-high heat.

2. Add the Thai curry paste to the hot pan and cook for 2 to 3 minutes until it turns fragrant

3. Add the coconut flavoring and buttermilk to the pan. Mix thoroughly.

4. Pour the chicken stock now and bring it to a simmer.

5. Allow it to simmer for around 5 to 8 minutes and reduce the heat to low.

6. Add the salmon to the liquid and season it with salt and pepper.

7. Poach it for 5 minutes until completely cooked

8. Remove from heat and set aside.

9. Follow the instructions from the noodles packet and cook the noodles accordingly.

10. Divide the noodles among two or three soup bowls and place the salmon fillet on top of each noodle stack.

11. Now add the lime juice and fish sauce to the soup in the saucepan and mix well.

12. Pour the soup liquid over the noodles and salmon.

13. Garnish with spring onion, chopped coriander, and red chili.

14. Serve hot and enjoy!

Creamy Spinach Soup

Servings: 2 - 3

Ingredients:

- 15 ounces spinach (fresh or frozen)
- 2 cups vegetable or chicken stock
- 3 tablespoons cream (low-fat)
- 1 finely chopped medium onion
- 2 1/2 skimmed milk
- 2 finely chopped garlic cloves
- 1 teaspoon nutmeg (freshly grated)
- Zest of half a lemon (finely grated)
- 1 teaspoon olive oil
- Salt and pepper, to taste

Method:

1. Heat the oil in a saucepan over medium heat.

2. Add the garlic and onion to the hot oil and stir-fry for 6 minutes until tender and translucent. The raw smell of the garlic should go.

3. Pour the vegetable or chicken stock to the pan and let it simmer.

4. Now, pour the skimmed milk and allow it to simmer

5. Add half of the spinach and grated lemon zest to the pan.

6. Cover and let it simmer for 15 minutes until the spinach wilts.

7. Let it cool for 5 to 8 minutes

8. Pour this soup into a high-speed blender and blend on high for 30 seconds until creamy.

9. Now, add the remaining spinach and blend again for 45 seconds until you get a thick green smooth creamy texture

10. Pour the blended soup to the saucepan and reheat. Add nutmeg, pepper, and salt and mix thoroughly.

11. Transfer the soup to the bowl and add the cream. Mix well and serve hot. Enjoy!

Spicy Prawn Soup

Servings: 4

Ingredients:

- 7-ounce bag raw prawns (large ones)
- 10 ½ ounce bag crunchy stir-fry veggies (you can take a mix of vegetables of your choice)
- 10 1/2 ounces shirataki noodles
- 5 ounces sliced shiitake mushrooms
- 4 tablespoons buttermilk (low-fat)
- 4 drops coconut flavoring
- 1 teaspoon colza oil
- 1 cup fish or vegetable stock
- 2 tablespoons Thai green curry paste
- Salt and pepper, to taste

Method:
1. Heat the colza oil in a saucepan over medium heat
2. Add the veggies to the hot oil and stir-fry until crunchy.
3. Add the mushrooms and cook for 3 minutes. Transfer the mushroom-veggie mixture to a plate and set aside
4. Add the Thai curry and fry for a minute.
5. Now, add the coconut flavoring, fish or vegetable stock, and buttermilk to the fried curry
6. Mix well and bring it to boil. Add the required salt and pepper.
7. Now add the prawns and the noodles.
8. Reduce the heat and simmer for 5 to 6 minutes until the prawns are completely cooked.
9. Add the mushroom-veggie mixture and stir well until combined.
10. Transfer to the bowls and serve hot. Enjoy!

Chapter Eleven: Dukan Dessert Recipes

Cinnamon & Caramel Cheesecake

Servings: 4

Ingredients:

- 1 teaspoon cinnamon
- 2 eggs
- 1 teaspoon sugar-free caramel essence or sauce
- 17 1/2 ounces Philadelphia cheese (or any other low-fat soft cheese)
- 5 tablespoons sweetener
- 5 ounces Greek yogurt (or low-fat sour cream)
- 2 tablespoons cornstarch (do not add this ingredient if you are in attack phase)

Method:
1. Preheat oven to 350 degrees Fahrenheit
2. Take a large bowl and crack the eggs into it

3. Add the cheese, yogurt, cornstarch, and sweetener to the cracked eggs.
4. Mix the contents well until they are completely incorporated
5. Add the cinnamon and caramel essences to the mixture in the bowl
6. Line a baking tray with parchment paper and keep ready
7. Pour this mixture in a lined baking tray and bake for 45 minutes
8. Remove from oven and let it cool. Refrigerate overnight or for minimum 3 hours
9. Slice the cheesecake and serve chilled. Enjoy!

Yogurt Jelly with Rum, Vanilla, and Cinnamon

Servings: 2

Ingredients:

- 10 ounces Greek yogurt (fat-free)
- 3 to 4 drops rum essence
- 1 tablespoon vanilla
- 1/4 teaspoon cinnamon
- 3 tablespoons skimmed milk
- 6 gelatin leaves
- 4 tablespoons sweetener

Method:

1. Take a small bowl and place the gelatin leaves. Pour cold water over it until it is immersed. Let it soak for a while.
2. Pour milk in a small pot and bring it to a soft boil. Set aside.
3. Combine the yogurt, rum, vanilla, and sweetener in a medium bowl until the contents are mixed thoroughly
4. Take the gelatin leaves from the water and put it in the boiled milk. Stir so that the leaves dissolve.
5. Pour the yogurt-rum-vanilla mixture to the milk slowly as you continue stirring.
6. Transfer this mixture into a greased pan and refrigerate overnight or for 3 hours.
7. Sprinkle the cinnamon over the top before serving and enjoy!

Rum and Wolfberry Ice Cream

Servings: 3

Ingredients:

- 3 to 5 drops rum essence
- 2 tablespoons goji berry
- 6 tablespoons skimmed milk
- 21 ounces Greek yogurt (fat-free)
- 4 tablespoons powdered skim milk
- 4 tablespoons sweetener
- 1 egg yolk (optional)

Method:

1. Take a small bowl and place the goji berries in it.
2. Pour water over the berries until they submerge and then add the rum essence to it.
3. Stir once and let it sit for 5 minutes to hydrate.
4. Take another bowl and pour the skimmed milk into it.
5. Add the yogurt, skim milk powder, sweetener and the egg yolk to the milk.
6. Mix well until the contents blend well (no lumps).
7. Drain the goji berries from the rum-flavored water and add it to the milk mixture in the large bowl.
8. Mix them thoroughly until you get a smooth and creamy texture.
9. Cover the bowl with aluminum foil or plastic wrap and refrigerate overnight or for 8 hours (if you can refrigerate for 24 hours, it will be even better!)
10. Pour the chilled creamy mixture into freezer container of an electric ice cream maker and follow the manufacturer's instructions.

11. If you do not have an ice cream maker, uncover the bowl and place it in the freezer for 12 hours.
12. You will have to remove the bowl from the freezer four times during the period and whip directly on the mixture for 60 seconds.
13. Transfer the ice cream to a container and store in the freezer.
14. Serve whenever needed and enjoy!

Cinnamon Pudding

Servings: 2

Ingredients:

- 1/2 teaspoon ground cinnamon
- 1/2 cup cream cheese (fat-free)
- 1 tablespoon brown sugar
- 1/2 cup soft tofu
- 3 tablespoons sweetener
- 3/4 teaspoon vanilla extract

Method:

1. Take a high-speed blender and place the tofu in it.
2. Add the cream cheese, vanilla extract, and sweetener to the tofu in the blender
3. Blend on high for 30 seconds until smooth
4. Add the cinnamon and brown sugar to the blender, blend on high for 45 seconds until creamy and thick.
5. Transfer to a bowl and refrigerate for 4 to 6 hours until the pudding gets thicker.
6. Serve chilled and enjoy!

Triple Chocolate Pancakes

Servings: 2

Ingredients:

- 2 tablespoons chocolate syrup
- 4 tablespoons chocolate soy milk (low-fat)
- 1 egg
- 4 1/2 tablespoons oat bran
- 1 tablespoon cocoa powder
- 1/4 teaspoon baking powder
- 1 teaspoon vanilla extract
- Pinch of salt
- 1 packet of Splenda sweetener
- Nonstick cooking spray

Method:

1. Take a food processor or high-speed blender and place the oat bran in it.
2. Process the oat to a powder (should have the consistency of a flour powder)
3. Transfer the oat bran powder to a medium-sized bowl and add the salt, baking powder, cocoa powder, and Splenda. Mix the contents thoroughly.
4. Take another small bowl and crack the egg into it.
5. Add the chocolate soymilk and vanilla extract to the cracked egg.
6. Whisk them together until mixed well.
7. Pour the chocolate mixture into the oat mixture and mix thoroughly without any lumps.
8. Grease a nonstick frying pan with cooking spray and heat it on medium heat

9. Pour half the mixture into the hot pan and spread a bit to round shape (don't make it like a crepe, it should be thick round pancake)
10. Let it cook for 2 to 3 minutes until the edges become crisp and bubbles start forming in the center.
11. Add more cooking spray if required and flip the pancake.
12. Cook for another 2 minutes and transfer to a plate
13. Repeat steps 9 to 12 with the remaining mixture
14. Serve warm or cold and enjoy!

Flourless Cinnamon Bun

Servings: 2

Ingredients:

- 1/4 teaspoon ground cinnamon + extra
- 2 1/2 tablespoons half & half (fat-free)
- 4 packets Splenda
- 1/2 teaspoon vanilla extract
- 1/2 tablespoon cornstarch (ignore this ingredient if in attack phase)
- 4 tablespoons protein powder (unflavored)
- 1/2 teaspoon baking powder
- 1 tablespoon brown sugar

For the frosting
- 1 tablespoon half & half (fat-free)
- 2 packets Splenda
- 2 tablespoons cream cheese (fat-free)
- 2 tablespoons skim milk

Method:
1. Mix together the cinnamon, half & half cream, Splenda, vanilla extract, cornstarch, protein powder, baking powder and brown sugar in a bowl.
2. The mixture should be smooth and creamy.
3. Fill 1/3rd of the soufflé cup with this smooth mixture (if you have the mixture remaining, pour to few more cups)
4. Microwave this for 30 to 45 seconds and then let it sit for a minute or two
5. For the frosting, heat a small saucepan over low heat.

6. Add the half & half, Splenda, cream cheese and skim milk to the hot pan.
7. Let it cook while you keep stirring constantly until the cheese melts.
8. Once the contents and the flavors are completely blended, turn off the heat.
9. Pour the frosting over the cups and sprinkle with a bit of cinnamon.
10. Serve immediately and enjoy!

Chocolate Chip Dip

Servings: 2

Ingredients:

- 1/2 tablespoon egg whites
- 1 teaspoon skim milk
- 1 1/2 tablespoon cocoa powder
- 1/4 teaspoon vanilla extract
- 7 packets Splenda
- Pinch of salt

For the dip
- 1/2 cup cream cheese (fat-free)
- 1 tablespoon Splenda brown sugar
- 1/2 cup firm tofu
- 3/4 teaspoon vanilla extract
- 3 packets Splenda

Method:

1. Preheat the oven to 350 degrees Fahrenheit
2. Blend together the egg whites, skim milk, cocoa powder, vanilla extract, Splenda and salt in a high-speed blender or mixer for 45 seconds until smooth and creamy.
3. Line a baking tray with parchment paper and spoon the chocolate mixture into the tray.
4. Make a neat 2-inch circle with the chocolate mixture and bake for 8 to 10 minutes
5. Remove from the oven and immediately place it in a freezer.
6. Let it sit there for 5 to 8 minutes to harden.

7. Remove from the freezer and cut the chocolate into a small square (or whatever shape you prefer for your chocolate chips). Set aside

8. To make the chocolate dip, blend the cream cheese, brown sugar, tofu, and vanilla extract in a high-speed blender for 60 seconds until creamy and thick.

9. Transfer the dip to a bowl and add the prepared chocolate chips into it. Mix well

10. Serve chilled and enjoy!

Pumpkin Pie Custard

Servings: 10

Ingredients:

- 2 cups canned pumpkin
- 1/2 cup skim milk
- 8 egg whites
- 1/4 teaspoon nutmeg (ground)
- 1 can evaporated milk (fat-free)
- 1 teaspoon cinnamon (ground)
- 5 tablespoons sweetener
- 1/2 teaspoon ginger (ground)
- 1/4 teaspoon salt
- 1/4 teaspoon cloves (ground)
- Nonstick cooking spray

Method:

1. Take a large bowl and pour the egg whites into it.
2. Add the pumpkin, skim milk, and evaporated milk to the egg white.
3. Beat them all together until you get a smooth and creamy consistency
4. Preheat the oven to 350 degrees Fahrenheit.
5. Grease the 10 ramekins (6-ounce size) with cooking spray
6. Spoon the mixture into these greased ramekins and bake for 45 minutes.
7. The mixture should be baked well enough for an inserted knife (in the center) to come out clean.
8. Once baked, remove from the oven and let it cool.
9. Refrigerate for 3 to 4 hours before serving.
10. Serve chilled and enjoy!

Gingerbread Biscotti

Servings: 4 to 6

Ingredients:

- 3/4 cup oat bran
- 2 tablespoons skim milk
- 2 tablespoons Splenda brown sugar
- 1/2 teaspoon vanilla extract
- 2 teaspoon cocoa powder
- 1/4 teaspoon baking soda
- 1 teaspoon cinnamon
- 1/4 teaspoon ginger (ground)
- 1/8 teaspoon salt
- 2 packets Splenda
- Cooking spray

Method:

1. Preheat oven at 375 degrees Fahrenheit.
2. Blend together the oat bran, brown sugar, cocoa powder, baking soda, cinnamon, ginger, salt, and Splenda in a food processor or high-speed blender.
3. Transfer the mixture to a medium-sized bowl and add the vanilla extract and skim milk to it.
4. Spray a bit of cooking spray into the mixture and combine the ingredients together.
5. Line a parchment paper on a baking tray and keep ready.
6. Spoon the mixture to the baking tray and form biscotti-shaped cookies (you will be able to make six)
7. Bake this for 10 minutes until crispy
8. Turn off the oven and let it cool inside
9. Transfer to a bowl and serve immediately. Enjoy!

Chocolate Mousse

Servings: 4

Ingredients:

- 4 egg whites
- 1 1/2 tablespoons cocoa powder
- 4 egg yolks
- 1/2 teaspoon cream of tartar
- 9 packets of Splenda
- 1/2 cup boiling water
- 1 tablespoon gelatin
- 1 teaspoon vanilla extract

Method:

1. Pour the boiling water into a small ball and dissolve the gelatin in it.
2. Mix slowly and add the cocoa powder as you continue stirring
3. Refrigerate the mixture to cool
4. Beat together the egg whites and cream of tartar using an electric mixer or hand blender until peaks form
5. Now, add the Splenda to the mixture and continue to stir until you get a thick consistency.
6. Add the egg yolks one by one and mix thoroughly before you add the next yolk. There shouldn't be any lumps, you should get a smooth consistency
7. Add the vanilla extract and mix well.
8. Continue stirring as you add the cocoa mixture slowly (be careful to avoid lumps)
9. When the mixture is completely smooth and creamy, pour it into soufflé cups and refrigerate for 4 to 6 hours until it sets.
10. Serve chilled and enjoy!

Oat Bran Muffins and Cinnamon

Servings: 6 muffins

Ingredients:

- 6 tablespoons oat bran
- 2 eggs
- 1 teaspoon cinnamon
- 1 teaspoon baking powder
- 6 tablespoons yogurt (zero-fat)
- 4 tablespoons sweetener.

Method:

1. Take a medium-sized bowl and mix together the oat bran, cinnamon, baking powder and sweetening thoroughly.
2. Crack the two eggs into the bowl and add yogurt.
3. Beat the mixture well until you get a smooth creamy mixture and add the sweetener to it.
4. Stir the mixture again and make sure you don't have any lumps.
5. Preheat the oven to 338 degrees Fahrenheit.
6. Pour the mixture into 6 muffin cups and bake for 20 minutes until soft and set.
7. Turn off the oven and let it cool.
8. Serve warm and enjoy!

Conclusion

We have come to the end of this book. I would like to take this opportunity to thank you once again for choosing this book.

The book has covered the primary objective, which is to give the readers a brief description of the Dukan Diet, the history behind it and its various phases.

The chapters give brief detailing of the foods to eat, a sample meal plan and also answers frequently asked questions. There are few chapters dedicated exclusively to delicious, easy and tasty vegetarian and non-vegetarian Dukan recipes. You can easily cook them and enjoy a delicious meal. It is necessary to have minimum 20 to maximum 30 minutes workout regimen daily to help your body in shedding that excess flab.

Try making your recipes more creative by adding your own mix and max combination of vegetables and protein sources to make cooking fun! I sincerely hope this book was useful and has helped in answering most of the queries you had in mind.

If you enjoyed the book, please consider leaving us a positive review on Amazon.

Recommended Reading

Dukan Diet: Lose Weight Fast and Lose Weight Forever

https://amzn.to/2CmvdIH

Dukan Diet: Attack Phase Meal Plan

https://amzn.to/2CljmdM

Self Esteem: Overcome Fear, Stress and Anxiety

https://amzn.to/2CNAFoO

Sources

https://www.dukandiet.com/low-carb-diet/4-phases

https://www.medicalnewstoday.com/articles/219612.php

https://www.bbcgoodfood.com/howto/guide/what-dukan-diet

https://www.webmd.com/diet/a-z/dukan-diet

https://www.healthline.com/nutrition/dukan-diet-101#section6

http://www.dukandiet.co.uk/getting-started

https://recipes.sparkpeople.com/recipe-detail.asp?recipe=389583

https://recipes.sparkpeople.com/recipe-detail.asp?recipe=1084368

https://recipes.sparkpeople.com/recipe-detail.asp?recipe=829921

https://recipes.sparkpeople.com/recipe-detail.asp?recipe=871899

https://recipes.sparkpeople.com/recipe-detail.asp?recipe=1726796

https://recipes.sparkpeople.com/recipe-detail.asp?recipe=1086516

https://recipes.sparkpeople.com/recipe-detail.asp?recipe=1697896

https://recipes.sparkpeople.com/recipe-detail.asp?recipe=340004

http://www.my-dukan-recipes.com/dukan-toast/

http://www.my-dukan-recipes.com/chicken-burger-dukan/

http://www.my-dukan-recipes.com/egg-white-frittata/

https://mydukandiet.com/recipes/oopsie-bread.html

https://mydukandiet.com/recipes/easy-meat-loaf.html

https://mydukandiet.com/recipes/rosemary-and-garlic-chicken.html

https://mydukandiet.com/recipes/scrambled-eggs-with-cream-cheese-and-chives.html

https://mydukandiet.com/recipes/egg-drop-soup.html

https://mydukandiet.com/recipes/roastbeef-and-mayo.html

https://mydukandiet.com/recipes/butterflied-chicken-breast-with-rosemary.html

http://www.drdukanrecipes.com/thai-beef-skewers/

http://www.drdukanrecipes.com/steamed-mussels-and-clams/

http://www.drdukanrecipes.com/spinach-quiche/

http://www.drdukanrecipes.com/spicy-lemon-roasted-chicken/

http://www.drdukanrecipes.com/proscuitto-wrapped-asparagus-with-egg/

http://www.drdukanrecipes.com/rosemary-grilled-chicken/

http://www.drdukanrecipes.com/slow-cookershredded-beef/

http://www.drdukanrecipes.com/spicy-lemon-roasted-chicken/

http://www.drdukanrecipes.com/steamed-cajun-shrimp/

http://www.drdukanrecipes.com/chive-pancakes/

http://www.drdukanrecipes.com/mini-mushroom-frittatas/

http://www.drdukanrecipes.com/broccoli-soup/

http://www.drdukanrecipes.com/eggplant-rollatini/

http://www.drdukanrecipes.com/chicken-lettuce-wraps/

https://mydukandiet.com/recipes/tomato-clafoutis.html

https://mydukandiet.com/recipes/king-prawn-lunch-delight.html

https://mydukandiet.com/recipes/chinese-style-tomato-egg-stir-fry.html

http://www.my-dukan-recipes.com/baked-chicken-with-cherry-tomatoes-and-peppers/

http://www.my-dukan-recipes.com/baked-chicken-with-vegetables/

https://mydukandiet.com/recipes/zero-carb-pizza.html

http://www.drdukanrecipes.com/curried-ground-beef/

http://www.drdukanrecipes.com/baked-buffalo-chicken-wings/

http://www.drdukanrecipes.com/mustard-egg-salad/

http://www.drdukanrecipes.com/collard-green-quiche/

https://mydukandiet.com/recipes/lemongrass-tofu-stirfry.html

https://mydukandiet.com/recipes/mexican-eggs.html

http://www.drdukanrecipes.com/asian-spicy-spaghetti-squash/

http://www.drdukanrecipes.com/middle-eastern-meatballs/

http://www.drdukanrecipes.com/simple-fish-ceviche/

http://www.drdukanrecipes.com/pepper-limechicken/

http://www.drdukanrecipes.com/baked-lemon-chicken-legs/

http://www.drdukanrecipes.com/cauliflower-soup/

http://www.drdukanrecipes.com/mushroom-omelet/

http://www.drdukanrecipes.com/deviled-eggs/

http://www.drdukanrecipes.com/crepe-quesadillas/

http://www.drdukanrecipes.com/ginger-salmon/

http://www.drdukanrecipes.com/cauliflower-rice/

http://www.drdukanrecipes.com/miso-soup/

http://www.drdukanrecipes.com/oat-bran-crackers/

https://mydukandiet.com/recipes/mint-curry-omelette.html

https://mydukandiet.com/recipes/meat-salad.html

http://www.my-dukan-recipes.com/creamy-mushroom-soup/

http://www.my-dukan-recipes.com/chicken-and-zucchini-moussaka/

http://www.my-dukan-recipes.com/category/recipes/consolidation-phase/

http://www.my-dukan-recipes.com/raspberry-cheesecake/

http://www.my-dukan-recipes.com/cinnamon-caramel-cheesecake/

http://www.my-dukan-recipes.com/yogurt-jelly-with-rum-vanilla-and-cinnamon/

http://www.my-dukan-recipes.com/rum-and-goji-ice-cream/

https://dukantopia.com/tag/dukan-dessert/

http://www.dukandiet.co.uk/other-menus/go-green

http://thedukandietsite.com/1094/dukan-diet-cruise-phase-recipes-cauliflower-mash/

http://thedukandietsite.com/1162/dukan-diet-cruise-phase-recipes-dukan-cauliflower-pizza/

http://thedukandietsite.com/2517/thanksgiving-on-the-dukan-diet-cruise-or-consolidation-phase/

http://thedukandietsite.com/1966/dukan-diet-cruise-phase-recipe-roasted-red-pepper-and-carrot-soup/

http://thedukandietsite.com/3357/dukan-diet-cruise-recipe-lumpy-dukan-miracle-soup/

http://thedukandietsite.com/3975/dukan-diet-recipe-baked-zucchini-chips-or-courgette-crisps/

http://www.dukandiet.co.uk/other-menus/go-crazy-for-soup

https://www.fitneass.com/dukan-diet/

https://www.dukandiet.com/weight-loss-coaching/menu-of-the-month/menulist/36

https://www.dukandiet.com/weight-loss-coaching/menu-of-the-month/menulist/37#main_dish_recipe

https://www.dukandiet.com/weight-loss-coaching/menu-of-the-month/menulist/34#main_dish_recipe

https://www.dukandiet.com/weight-loss-coaching/menu-of-the-month/menulist/33#main_dish_recipe

https://www.dukandiet.com/faq

Made in United States
Troutdale, OR
02/22/2024

17895971R10116